THE CROSSING:
THE ONLY RESPONSE
TO EXISTENTIAL RISK

THE CROSSING: THE ONLY RESPONSE TO EXISTENTIAL RISK

THE EIGHT INJUNCTIONS FROM HOMO SAPIENS TO HOMO AMOR

CROSSING OVER TO THE SIDE OF LOVE

. . .

One Mountain, Many Paths: Oral Essays
Volume Thirty-Seven

DR. MARC GAFNI

Author: Marc Gafni
Title: The Crossing: The Only Response to Existential Risk
Identifiers: ISBN 979-8-88834-086-8 (electronic)
ISBN 979-8-88834-085-1 (paperback)
Library of Congress Cataloging-in-Publication Data available

Edited by Talya Bloom and Krista Josepha Steenbergen

World Philosophy and Religion Press,
St. Johnsbury, VT

in conjunction with

IP Integral Publishers

https://worldphilosophyandreligion.org

JOIN THE REVOLUTION!

CONTENTS

CHAPTER 3   **HOMO AMOR INJUNCTION ONE:
LET YOUR HEART BE BROKEN**

CHAPTER 14   **HOMO AMOR INJUNCTION EIGHT:
COMMIT OUTRAGEOUS ACTS OF LOVE**

EDITORIAL NOTE ABOUT AUTHORSHIP, EDITING, AND THE RADICAL CONTEXT FOR THIS SERIES

THIS ORAL ESSAYS SERIES IS AN ENTRYWAY TO THE GREAT LIBRARY OF COSMOEROTIC HUMANISM

This Oral Essays series is part of the overarching project of the Great Library at the Center for World Philosophy and Religion, led by Dr. Marc Gafni, together with Dr. Zak Stein. The aim of the Great Library project is to articulate a robust and comprehensive new Story of Value, CosmoErotic Humanism, in the form of dozens of well-researched and extensively footnoted academic works.

Our vision is to provide the philosophical framework that will be vital for navigating humanity through this time of immense crisis and transformation.

To begin your journey into CosmoErotic Humanism, we tenderly refer you to the book *First Principles and First Values*, co-authored by Marc Gafni, Zak Stein, and Ken Wilber, under the name David J. Temple. David J. Temple is a pseudonym created for enabling ongoing collaborative authorship at the Center for World Philosophy and Religion. The two primary authors behind David J. Temple are Marc Gafni and Zak Stein, and for different projects, specific writers will be named as part of the collaboration, such as Ken Wilber and others.

Three other volumes complete this introduction: *A Return to Eros*, by Marc Gafni and Kristina Kincaid; *Your Unique Self*, by Marc Gafni; and *Education in a Time between Worlds*, by Zak Stein.

We hope that the Oral Essays in the present volume, with their informal style of transmission, will serve as an allurement and entryway for you into the more formal books of the Great Library that provide the robust intellectual underpinnings of the new Story of Value.

A NOTE ABOUT THE EDITORS

This Oral Essays collection has been edited by students of the new Story of CosmoErotic Humanism. Each of us has actively participated in *One Mountain, Many Paths*, and most of us have been in deep "Holy of Holies" study with Dr. Marc Gafni for many years.

We have been privileged to find ourselves well-versed in the teachings, and even emerging as lineage-holders of CosmoErotic Humanism.[1]

---

1 CosmoErotic Humanism is a world philosophical movement aimed at reconstructing the collapse of value at the core of global culture. Much like Romanticism or Existentialism, CosmoErotic Humanism is not merely a theory but a movement that changes the very mood of Reality. It is an invitation to participate in evolving the source code of consciousness and culture towards a cosmocentric *ethos* for a planetary civilization.

The term CosmoErotic Humanism, initially coined by Dr. Gafni and colleagues, points to a complex, multi-faceted, layered, and nuanced evolutionary set of insights that has evolved over decades of intensive research, teaching, and spiritual practice from deep within a wide range of wisdom traditions (including the Wisdom of Solomon lineage tradition, Bodhisattva Buddhism, and Kashmir Shaivism), as well as multiple disciplines including complexity theory, chaos theory, emergence theory, molecular biology, and the more classical disciplines of the humanities.

The seeds of CosmoErotic Humanism were planted with Dr. Marc Gafni's work on a two-volume, 1,000-page opus called *Radical Kabbalah* (Integral Publishers, 2012). This scholarly work, sourced from deep study within the esoteric lineage texts of the Wisdom of Solomon, points to a non-dual, or acosmic, realization which—unlike the prevailing conceptualization of non-duality—does not efface the human being; rather, it is highly

We view this editing project as a privilege and a deep practice of study and clarification. We experience ourselves as a *mystical editing society*, frequently meeting and conversing together about the content—the depth of knowledge and wisdom offered here—as well as the technical intricacies involved with publishing a beautiful and coherent series of books. In so doing, we function as a "Unique Self Symphony," which itself is a Dharmic term that connotes an omni-considerate collaboration between realized Unique Selves synergizing our unique gifts into a new emergence greater than the sum of the parts. Even as we worked diligently to standardize our editing styles, meeting on a weekly basis to debate the nuances of phrasing, we also operated from within a deep appreciation of the unique style that each editor brought to his or her work. As such, the reader might notice some variation in editing style among the books.

Please note that Dr. Marc Gafni has not reviewed these edited Oral Essays, as he is deeply engaged in writing the formal books of the Great Library. But he has been generous in responding to questions and providing overall guidance in the project. Overall, as Marc's students and students of the *dharma*, we have made it a key project at the Center to publish these pieces of work relatively independently.

OUR UNIQUE ORAL-ESSAY EDITING STYLE PRESERVES THE ENERGY OF THE ORIGINAL TRANSMISSION

Dr. Marc Gafni is a uniquely gifted teacher whose oral transmission is imbued with a quality that has proven transformative for his students. Many

---

humanistic in its nature. The next step in the evolution of CosmoErotic Humanism was the insight that all of Reality is evolving Eros, which lives in, as, and through the human being. A failure of Eros leads inexorably to the creation of narratives of "pseudo-eros." CosmoErotic Humanism is a response to the modern mental and social breakdown sourced in the proliferation of multiple forms of pseudo-eros and its broken narratives, such as rivalrous conflict governed by win/lose metrics and the dogmatic denial of intrinsic value in Cosmos, which together generate our current "global intimacy disorder."

of us feel mystically transformed by both the content and the underlying energy of the transmission style. Therefore, as we like to say, *trust the magic ways the dharma comes through your unique understanding!*

As Marc's empowered students, colleagues, and beloved friends, we have a deep knowing that these teachings are vital for the survival and thriving of humanity as we know it, and we recognize the importance of publishing his teachings in a written format that will be accessible by future generations. At the same time, we sought to preserve the Eros of the original oral transmission with all of its nuance, power, and depth. Our intention in the editing process, to the greatest extent possible, has been to keep these spoken artifacts intact in order to maintain the flow of the original transmission. We have therefore chosen not to engage in intensive formal editing, as we found that doing so resulted in the loss of the energetic transmission that is so key to fully receiving the *dharma.*

After experimenting with many ways to present these texts, we developed a specific way of laying out the text on the page. Marc, in collaboration with Zak Stein and Russian intellectual/artist Elena Maslova-Levin—and ultimately all of the editors, through many conversations—developed a unique, artistic presentation of the text, using bolding, italics, bullet points, and other stylistic features which together serve to accentuate the immediacy of the oral transmission.

As part of this editing style, intended to preserve the integrity of the original transmission, we have refrained from removing the frequent recapitulations of key themes. We found that each recapitulation contributes something vital to the rhythm and music beneath the words, like the beating drum of our hearts. These recapitulations not only review previous material but also add important new emphases, perspectives, and elements of the new Story of Value. We ask for your patience as a reader to trust the rhythm of these texts, and we trust you as a reader to have the depth and steadiness to find your way through.

THE INVITATION

We invite you to find your way into this revolution. Each one of our Unique Selves and unique gifts are desperately needed as we co-create this new Story of Value together, as part of the covenant between generations, for the sake of the whole.

Let's *play a larger game* and evolve the very source code of consciousness and culture together.

With mad love,

The Editors

LOVE OR DIE

LOCATING OURSELVES: ARTICULATING THE ESSENTIAL CONTEXT FOR THE ONE MOUNTAIN, MANY PATHS ORAL ESSAYS

SETTING OUR INTENTION

Intention setting is everything.

We're here—as da Vinci was with his cohort in the Renaissance—**to play a larger game, to participate in the evolution of love, which is to tell the new Story of Value rooted in First Principles and First Values.**

- Our intention is to recognize the critical historical juncture in which we find ourselves.
- Our intention is to take our seat at the table of history and to say, *we take responsibility for this.*
- Our intention is to participate as revolutionaries for the sake of the whole.

What we're here to do is revolution; revolution for the sake of the evolution of love.

It's a revolution for the sake of the trillions of unborn lives that will not manifest:

- The unborn loves

- The unborn creativity
- The unborn goodness
- The unborn truth
- The unborn beauty

All of it looks to us.

Not because we're engaged in grandiosity. Not at all!

- We're trembling before She.
- We're trembling with joy at the privilege.
- We're trembling with joy at the responsibility.
- We're trembling with joy at the Possibility of Possibility.
- We have to enact a new story in this moment of time. Because it is only a new story that can change the vector of history.

The most revolutionary act that we can do—the greatest moral imperative of this time—**is to articulate a new story at this time between worlds and this time between stories**.

Story is not made up, as postmodernity suggests. **We all live in inescapable frameworks; our framework is the story we live in.** Right now, Reality lives according to win/lose metrics, a story that is generating existential risk. **We need to change that story.**

When we change that story, when we tell a new story—not a made-up story, but a new Story of Value, rooted in First Principles and First Values—**then it all changes.**

We need to participate in the evolution of the source code of consciousness and culture, which is the evolution of love.

It's the most important, exciting, evolutionary, revolutionary act that we can do to alleviate suffering: to be lovers.

Like Rumi, the great poet of Sufism, we have to be "mad lovers," because it's the only sanity.

To be mad lovers is to see around the corner, to not be so obsessed with the details of the contractions of my life.

Let me see bigger.

Let me take complete care of myself in every possible way, let me completely attend to those in my circle of intimacy and influence, and then—*let me expand my circle.*

That's what we're here for.

- Our intention is to participate in the *LoveForce*, the *LoveIntelligence*, the *LoveBeauty*, the *LoveDesire* that literally animates Cosmos all the way up and all the way down.
- Our intention is to participate in the evolution of love.

[In the next few pages we will cover some key concepts which are essential to locating ourselves and setting the context for all the One Mountain, Many Paths Oral Essays. —Eds.]

OVERVIEW: EROS IS NO LONGER A LUXURY—IT'S LOVE OR DIE

Eros is life.

The failure of Eros destroys life.

Our lack of Eros is poised to destroy the world.

All civilizations have fallen because the stories that they lived in were, in some sense, stories based on rivalrous conflict governed by win/lose metrics. Every civilization was weakened by interior polarization caused by the lack of a shared Story of Value.

We now have a global civilization, but we haven't created a shared Story of Value.

We haven't solved the generator functions that caused all civilizations to fall. Our global civilization has exponential technologies and extraction models depleting the Earth of resources that took billions of years to create, which is going to lead to a civilizational collapse.

Existential risk is risk to our very existence.

The choice is clear: love or die.

It's that simple.

Eros is no longer a luxury. It is an absolute necessity for the survival of the individual and the planet.

In the last half a century, modern psychology has documented an age-old truth: a fully nourished baby who is not held in loving arms will die.

So too, our world, both personal and global—even with all the resources of intelligence and technology at our disposal—will die without being held in love, in the embrace of Eros.

We must embrace a personal path of love and a global politics of love.

Not ordinary love. Not love which is "mere human sentiment," but Eros, or what we sometimes call Outrageous Love, which is the heart of existence itself.

We live in a world of outrageous pain.

The only response is Outrageous Love.

WHAT IS EROS?

Eros is the experience of radical aliveness, moving towards, seeking, desiring ever deeper contact and ever greater wholeness.[2] Eros is

---

2 We define Eros through what we refer to as the Eros equation (one of a series of what we call interior science equations):

the core fabric of Reality's being and the motivational architecture of Reality's becoming.

Eros is what animates the evolutionary impulse itself, from the very inception of Cosmos all the way to our very selves, who awaken to the realization that the evolutionary impulse throbs uniquely in each of us.

The realization of human awakening and transformation that lies at the core of the interior sciences is the invitation—or even the urgent and desperate demand—of a madly loving Cosmos animated by infinities of power and infinities of intimacy.

The demand—the desperate invitation, the plea, the tender and fierce command of Cosmos that lives inside every human being—is to awaken: to awaken to our true nature as unique incarnations of Eros and Ethos that are needed and desperately desired by All-That-Is. Said slightly differently: Reality is Eros. Or: God is Eros.

The failure of Eros destroys life. The collapse of Eros is always the hidden (or not so hidden) root cause for the collapse of ethics.

This is true both personally and collectively. We live in a moment of a worldwide and personal collapse of Eros. Our lack of Eros is poised to destroy the world. Humanity is currently experiencing what has come to be known as existential risk, a risk to our very existence, or what I will refer to as the Second Shock of Existence.

Eros = Radical Aliveness x Desiring (Growing + Seeking) x Deeper Contact x Greater Wholeness x Self Actualization/Self Transcendence (Creation [Destruction])

There are good reasons for the formal language of the interior science equations in these writings, and the reader is invited to explore them on their own, in particular, in our work, David J. Temple, *First Principles and First Values: Forty-Two Propositions on CosmoErotic Humanism, the Meta-Crisis, and the World to Come* (World Philosophy and Religion, 2024).

EXISTENTIAL RISK: THE SECOND SHOCK OF EXISTENCE

The first shock of existence is the death of the human being—the realization that we will die, which dawns in human consciousness at the beginning of history. We are not talking about the biological fact of death but the *existential* realization of death. Although the interior sciences disclose that death is a portal between two days (there is vast empirical,[3] philosophical,[4] and anthro-ontological evidence[5] for the continuity of consciousness[6]), death is also, in our own direct surface experience, a stark end. And that is obviously not a bug but a feature in the system.

---

3   We refer to evidence gathered by the most serious of researchers, beginning with Henry and Edith Sedgwick at Cambridge University and William James at Harvard University, and continuing in highly rigorous form for the last 150 years, as recapitulated by Whiteheadian scholar David Ray Griffin in multiple volumes. See also, for example, Dean Radin, *Real Magic: Unlocking Your Natural Psychic Abilities to Create Everyday Miracles* (Potter/TenSpeed/Harmony, 2018), *The Conscious Universe: The Scientific Truth of Psychic Phenomena* (HarperCollins, 2010), and other books. Or see the earlier classic by Frederic William Henry Myers, *Human Personality and Its Survival of Bodily Death* (Longmans, Green, 1907).

4   This requires a cogent analysis of materialism and dualism, and the introduction of the far more cogent third possibility which we have called "pan-interiority."

5   We discuss Anthro-Ontology in some depth in *First Principles and First Values*, and see also the fuller conversation in David J. Temple, *First Principles and First Values: Towards an Evolving Perennialism: Introducing the Anthro-Ontological Method*—both published by World Philosophy and Religion Press, in Conjunction with Integral Publishers. For now, we will simply define it as an "innate and clear interior gnosis directly available to the human being."

6   See Dr. Marc Gafni and Dr. Zachary Stein's essay in preparation, "Beyond Death: Anthro-Ontology, Philosophy, and Empiricism." This essay is slated to appear in the book *Towards a World Religion: Homo Amor Essays*. The essay is also the ground for a larger book by the same authors, *Twelve Portals to Life Beyond Death: Responding to the Second Shock of Existence,* in which we discuss three forms of material: the empirical, the philosophical, and the anthro-ontological, and show how each form discredits the notion of death as the end.

Our first-person experience is that death ends this life. It is not the *totality* of our experience if we go deeper inside, but it is obviously intended to be the central, potent, and painful dimension of every human life. Indeed, as Ernest Becker potently reminded us, the denial of death is at our peril.

All the stories and all the plotlines and all the threads of living end at that moment. Whatever happens beyond, we have an actual experience of ending. **Paradoxically, that ending, the experience of the finality of mortality, is what presses us into life.** From the implicit demand of the first shock of existence, human beings were activated and pressed into creative emergence, and what emerged was all of human culture, both interior and exterior.

The second shock of existence is the realization of the potential death of all humanity. After all the stages of human history—matter, life, and mind in all of their stages of evolutionary unfolding—we have come to this place in the evolution of humanity, in which the gap between our exponentially expanding exterior technologies and our stalled (or even regressing) interior technologies of value has created dire catastrophic and existential risks.

This gap generates extraction models and exponential growth curves, rivalrous conflicts based on win/lose metrics, tragedies of the commons, and multipolar traps, in which everyone has to keep producing to the nth degree, including weaponized exponential threats to our very existence because we are afraid that the other parties are going to do it and not be transparent—hide it from us and then dominate us.

GENERATOR FUNCTIONS FOR EXISTENTIAL RISK

Let's outline clearly the main *generator functions for existential risk.*

Rivalrous conflicts governed by zero-sum, win/lose metrics. Rivalrous conflicts generate extraction models at the core of the economic system and exponential growth curves. Both of these drive and are driven by a contrived system of artificially manufactured desires and needs, delivered into culture by ever more precise forms of micro-targeting to individuals and groups through the ever more immersive environment of the internet.

Next, rivalrous conflicts and exponential growth curves animated by win/lose metrics generate **complicated, fragile world systems** highly vulnerable to myriad forms of collapse. Fragile local systems are made exponentially more fragile on a global level by our inability to meet global challenges with social, legal, political, economic, and ethical infrastructures that remain largely local.

All of this is a direct result of the failure to develop more adequate interior technologies that would be sufficiently compelling to displace "rivalrous conflict governed by win/lose metrics" as the motivational architecture for the human life world.

This failure has led to the conditions that will cause the implosion of systems that are already and quite literally on the brink of collapsing themselves. That's what we mean by the *second shock of existence.*

To recapitulate: the second shock of existence is not the death of the human being, but the potential death of humanity.

It is the *Death Star* moment of our species.

THE DECONSTRUCTION OF INTRINSIC VALUE

We stand in this moment poised between utopia and dystopia, at a time between worlds and a time between stories. We need a new Story of Value, eternal yet evolving, rooted in First Principles and First Values, which would become a universal grammar of value and a context for our diversity.

This is exactly what the Renaissance was. It was a time between worlds and a time between stories. In the Renaissance, we had been recently challenged by the Black Death, a pandemic that swept across Europe. The Black Death destroyed between a third to half of Europe and a huge part of

Asia. People died horrifically, brutally, in the streets. They had no idea how to meet this challenge, and so, in response to the Black Death, da Vinci and Ficino and their cohorts understood that they had to tell a new Story of Value.

That story was the story of modernity. Did they get it right?

- They got part of it right, which birthed, to use Jürgen Habermas' phrase, "the dignities of modernity," such as new ways of gathering information and universal human rights.
- But they also deconstructed the source of Value. They lost the basis for the Good, the True, and the Beautiful.

The basis used to be divine revelation: *God told us.* But this claim was owned by religion, and every religion began to overreach and over-claim. The revelation was thus often mediated through cultural categories and wasn't fully accurate.

Modernity threw out revelation, but was unable to establish a new basis for value.

Value was just assumed to be real. As it says in the founding document of the American Revolution: *We hold these truths to be self-evident*—that is, *we don't really have a basis for value; we just take it as a given.*

In other words, modernity took out a loan of social capital from the traditional world. The source of value was never worked out.

And then, gradually, value began to collapse.

- The Universe Story began to collapse.
- The belief that the Good, the True, and the Beautiful are real began to collapse.
- The belief that Love is real began to collapse.

As Bertrand Russell is reported to have said, "I cannot see how to refute the arguments for the subjectivity of ethical values, but I find myself incapable of believing that all that is wrong with wanton cruelty is that I do not like it."

What do you do if you grew up in a world in which value is not real? A world without a source of value, without a Universe Story, without a story of human identity, without a story of desire, without a narrative of power?

In the words of W.B. Yeats, *the center does not hold*.

- You have a collapse at the very center of society, because you no longer have Eros.
- You no longer have a Reality in which value is real, and so you have this lingering sense of emptiness.
- You have a complete collapse at the very center.
- We become *the hollow men and the stuffed men*, gesture without form.

And that's the source of our current existential risk.

THE DEEPER ROOT CAUSE OF THE META-CRISIS: A GLOBAL INTIMACY DISORDER

Above, I have outlined the major generator functions of existential risk. But there is a deeper cause for the existential risk that lurks underneath the rivalrous conflict governed by win/lose metrics and the fragile systems they engender.

And we cannot take the Death Star down without discerning and addressing this. We have already alluded to this root cause above, but at this point we need to make it more explicit so that, from this context, the adequate root response will become clear.

Modernity threw out the revelation, but was unable to establish a new basis for value.

This ostensibly surprising statement can be understood in a few simple steps:

1. All of the catastrophic and existential risk challenges we face are global: from climate change to artificial intelligence, pandemics, systems collapse, and exponential arms races.
2. Every global challenge self-evidently requires a global solution.
3. Global solutions can only be implemented with global co-ordination.
4. Global co-ordination is impossible without global coherence.
5. Global coherence is only possible if there is a global resonance between the parts.
6. Global resonance is only possible if we have global intimacy.

ONLY A SHARED STORY OF VALUE CAN GENERATE GLOBAL INTIMACY

Global intimacy—just like intimacy in a couple—is only possible when there is a shared story.

Not just a shared history, but a shared Story of Value.

- It is only a shared global story that can generate a new emergent quality of intimacy: global intimacy.
- A shared Story of Value must be rooted in shared ordinating values, or what we have called evolving First Values and First Principles.
- Intimacy requires a shared grammar of value as a matrix for a shared Story of Value.

The global intimacy disorder is the root cause for existential risk. The global intimacy disorder underlies the core generator functions for existential risk.

The global intimacy disorder is rooted in the failure to experience ourselves in a field of shared intrinsic value. This failure derives from the deconstruction of value.

Indeed, it is wholly accurate to say that **the root cause of the two generator functions of existential risk is the failed story of intrinsic value, or what we might also call the breakdown of Eros.**

1. The first generator function is **the success story**. Our modern success story is rivalrous conflict governed by win/lose metrics, which violates all the terms of the Intimacy Equation: there is no shared identity and no mutuality of recognition, feeling, value or purpose, and instead of *relative* otherness, there is *alienated* otherness. Such a story generates complicated fragile systems with no allurement or intimacy between the parts, systems which optimize for efficiency (as an expression of win/lose metrics) and not for resiliency and life.

2. The second generator function is **the deconstruction of intrinsic value** itself. The deconstruction of value is the sense that human value does not participate in the intrinsic value of the Real, for the Real is dogmatically declared to have no intrinsic value. Thus, there is no shared identity between the interior of the human being and Reality. There is no common participation in a field of shared intrinsic value. Instead of being intimate with value, we are alienated from value. And only intrinsic value can arouse will: political, moral, and social will.

To sum up, without a shared grammar of value there is no global intimacy, and therefore no global coherence, and no global coordination in response to catastrophic and existential risk, which means, put simply, there will be, quite literally, no future.

HEALING THE GLOBAL INTIMACY DISORDER
REQUIRES THE EVOLUTION OF INTIMACY

But we are not hopeless. On the contrary, we are filled with great hope. Hope is a memory of the future. That memory of the future *is* the direct hit that takes down the Death Star, the culture of death. **The direct hit must be**—as it has always been in history—**the emergence of a new stage of evolution.**

Crisis is an evolutionary driver, and every crisis is, at its core, a crisis of intimacy: from the oxygen crisis of the single cells dying which generated multicellular life at the dawn of existence, to the existential risk in this very moment.[7]

The direct hit is therefore structurally self-evident: the evolution of intimacy itself.

What is intimacy, as a structure of Cosmos all the way down and all the way up the evolutionary chain? We engage this inquiry in depth in other writings, but for now we will simply adduce what we have called the "Intimacy Equation":

> *Intimacy = shared identity in the context of [relative] otherness x mutuality of recognition x mutuality of pathos x mutuality of value x mutuality of purpose*

Intimacy is about the capacity of parts to generate a *shared identity* while retaining their otherness, or distinct identity. This requires multiple mutualities, including recognition, pathos (or feeling), value, and purpose. The parts must recognize and feel each other, even as they share value and purpose. But all of this must lead to intimate union—and not pathological

---

7 We demonstrate this principle in some depth in the multi-volume series, *The Universe: A Love Story* (forthcoming) (https://worldphilosophyandreligion.org/early-ontologies), *The Intimate Universe: Global Intimacy Disorder as Cause for Global Action Paralysis* (forthcoming), and in other writings of CosmoErotic Humanism.

fusion, where the distinct identity of the parts disappears—like subatomic particles that successfully become an atom, or two people who successfully become a couple.

THE DECONSTRUCTION OF VALUE IS THE DECONSTRUCTION OF INTIMACY

We have identified the global intimacy disorder as the root cause of the existential risk. But the underlying ultimate failure of intimacy is the deconstruction of value itself.

The deconstruction of value means that human value does not participate in any sense of intrinsic value of the Real. This is not about individual *values,* but about *the Field of Value* that underlies all of them. **When the human being**—moved, often sincerely or even nobly, by myriad cultural, historical, and psychological confusions—**claims to have stepped out of the Field of Value, then intimacy itself is deconstructed.**

The deconstruction of value is the deconstruction of intimacy.

In the absence of a shared Story of Value, a story that is an authentic expression of Reality's Eros, a story rooted in *pseudo-Eros* takes center stage and becomes the generator function for existential risk. Our modern pseudo-Eros story is *rivalrous conflict governed by win/lose metrics.* Such a story catalyzes in its wake the second generator function of existential risk: *complicated fragile systems with no allurement or intimacy between the parts.* It is in that sense that we have argued that the first generator function for existential risk is the success story.

- ◆ The failure of intimacy is precisely the impotent experience that there is no shared identity between the interior of the human being and Reality. **There is no shared identity in the sense of any kind of common participation in a field of shared intrinsic value.**
- ◆ **But only a shared Story of Value can arouse the global will**

required to engage catastrophic and existential risk. For it is only global political, moral, and social will—and we can even say *erotic* will—that can generate the most Good, True and Beautiful world that we have always known is possible.

THE EVOLUTION OF LOVE IS THE TELLING OF A NEW STORY

Coupled with the Intimacy Equation is the scientifically grounded realization, in both the exterior and interior sciences, that Reality is a progressive deepening of intimacies, or, said slightly differently:

Reality is Evolution. Evolution is the evolution of intimacy.

- ◆ The evolution of intimacy requires—both personally and collectively—a deeper, more accurate discernment of the nature of our universe, ourselves, and our beloveds.
- ◆ This new discernment generates a new global Story of Value.
- ◆ The new global Story of Value generates an emergent, heretofore unseen global intimacy and heals the global intimacy disorder.

The new Story of Value is the direct hit that takes down the Death Star and replaces it with the hope that invokes the memory of our best future.

Global intimacy facilitates global coherence, which facilitates global coordination, which activates the possibility of our creative and effectively coordinated global responses to the global meta-crisis in its entirety and its specific expressions.

To solve Bertrand Russell's challenge—the apparent argument for the subjectivity of ethical values—**we have to reground value theory in eternal yet evolving First Principles and First Values, and articulate a new Story of Value.**

This is what we call CosmoErotic Humanism.

CosmoErotic Humanism—together with other emergent strands—**needs to become the ground of a world religion as a context for our diversity**. We need religion, even as we need science, to articulate a shared global grammar of value.

As we said at the beginning, our choice is simple: love or die.

- To love means to participate in the evolution of love, which is the evolution of the human Story of Value.
- To love means to evolve and activate a new cultural enlightenment—rooted in a new narrative of identity, a new narrative of value, a new narrative of intimate communion, a new narrative of desire, a new narrative of power—all of which will birth new narratives of economics and politics.
- The evolution of love is the telling of a new story.

The new story that must be told is a love story, for in fact that is the deepest truth of Reality, rooted in the best exterior and interior sciences, that we have at this moment in time:

- Reality is not merely a fact. Reality is a story.
- Reality is not an ordinary story. Reality is a love story.
- Reality is not an ordinary love story. Reality is an Outrageous Love Story.

Story doesn't mean it's *made-up*.

It means doing the hard work of integrating the validated insights of the traditional world, the modern world, and the postmodern world.

This is the intention at the heart of telling the new Story of CosmoErotic Humanism.

ABOUT THIS VOLUME

THE CROSSING IS THE ONLY VIABLE RESPONSE TO THE SECOND SHOCK OF EXISTENCE

The first shock of existence is the realization at the dawn of human aware-ness that "the skull grins in at the banquet." Life is confronted by death. The first shock of existence is the death of the individual human being.

The second shock of existence is the realization of the potential death of humanity, or in a second form, the death of our humanity.

The experience of the second shock is rooted in the realization that all civilizations have fallen because the stories that they lived in were, in some sense, based on rivalrous conflict governed by win/lose metrics.

Every civilization was weakened by interior polarization caused by the lack of a shared Story of Value. Without a depth of shared value, the natural fault lines of rivalrous conflict fractured the commons and felled all civilizations.

We now have a global civilization, but we haven't created a corresponding Story of Value to address the worldwide meta-crisis. We haven't solved the generator functions that cause all civilizations to fall.

Moreover, our global civilization has generated exponential technologies and extraction models, depleting the Earth of resources that took billions of years to form. This may lead to a civilizational collapse—which in a global context means either the death of humanity or the death of *our* humanity.

Without a shared universal grammar of value—rooted in First Principles and First Values and grounded in a Story of Value to serve as a context for our diversity—the human family will fragment and eventually self-destruct. It is only an evolution of the source code of culture and consciousness itself—a kind of crossing over to the next level of human emergence—that can respond to the meta-crisis of our time. The Crossing is the only viable response to the second shock of existence: the potential death of humanity or the death of our humanity.

FROM CRISIS TO CROSSING

We choose the term "crossing" with some degree of trembling intention. The phrase derives from the philology and collective memory of the interior sciences of Hebrew wisdom. Indeed, the very word "Hebrew" derives from the words "eber" or "ever" meaning crossing. The word is in reference therefore to Abraham, known also as Ibrahim. These interior sciences texts, imagining the Euphrates River that wound through the fertile crescent, declaim, "the entire world is one side and Abraham crosses over to the other side." The Hebrew refers to the one who crosses to the other side. In the axial traditions of the West and East, Abraham is recognized as being a seminal hero of human history, an early adopter of *Homo amor*.

But the language play is even more potent and precise. The words Hebrew and crossing—in the Hebrew language—contain the same three letter root as the word for past. The implication of the text is that Abraham himself archetypally incarnates a time between worlds and a time between stories.

Abraham, in the language of one interior science text, "goes forth to himself"—he crosses over from the memory of the past to the memory of the future. Abraham is the boundary crosser who breaks the tyranny of yesterday to create a possible tomorrow. Abraham is the hero whose heart, body, and mind are coded with memories of the future.

We must become the Abraham of today.

THE CROSSING: BECOMING *HOMO AMOR*

In this time between worlds and time between stories, we cross over together.

In response to the second shock of existence, which is the potential death of humanity or the death of our humanity, we must cross over from *Homo sapiens* to *Homo amor*.

The Crossing, at its core, is crossing over from one side (where there are always two sides fighting each other) to the other side (where's only one side—that's the side of love).

In this book, we go through the eight injunctions of *Homo amor*:

1. Let your heart be broken.
2. Cry from one side of the mouth, laugh from the other.
3. Your story matters.
4. Take care of unfinished business.
5. Take the red pill.
6. Live your story.
7. Take your unique risk.
8. Commit Outrageous Acts of Love.

This book is compiled from lightly edited transcriptions from The Crossing, an event originally initiated and organized and facilitated by James Bampfield.

The event took place in Holland in 2024. The larger context for the Crossing was a series of more than thirty Wisdom School and Mystery School events that preceded this event.

The intention of The Crossing is a template for the evolutionary transformation from *Homo sapiens* to *Homo amor*—which is both the overwhelming joy and most urgent global need at this moment of meta crisis.

The Crossing continues to deepen as an evolving template for the transformative initiation into becoming the new human and the new humanity. It is a rite of passage that can and must be replicated across the world—each location in its own vernacular of spirit and culture; its own unique quality of intimacy. It is only a world-wide explosion of people who refuse to settle, people willing to go all the way in this life time, to cross over and become the new human, that will be a sufficient response to the potential death of humanity and the potential death of our humanity.

Volume 37

These oral essays are edited talks delivered by Marc Gafni at The Crossing, a gathering that took place in Holland in 2024.

CHAPTER ONE

IF WE DON'T SUCCEED IN CROSSING OVER, WE WILL GO EXTINCT

EITHER CROSSING OR EXTINCTION

This book is not a personal development book—although things may be shared that catalyze development.

This is not a transformational book in the classical sense—although things may be shared that catalyze transformation.

I'm not going to say anything which is casual. It's not like, *oh, just throw out something, or we read something in the newspaper, or we read a book someplace.*

The premise of *The Crossing* is validated by the most extensive cross-cultural data. If I make a claim, you can disagree with it, but you've got to really base it in something real—because I'm basing the claim on the best integration of pretty much all of the material in a particular vector available at this moment in history.

And the claim I'm about to make is so big it would be disrespectful and unloving to you, and it would be alienation between us if I made the claim without that level of validation. One of the groups in our constellation of work at the Center for World Philosophy and Religion has just finished an integration of all of the risk reports available today in the world—that is something we worked on in the last year.

The claim I'm going to make is a very sober claim and it's an ecstatic claim. And it's going to bring to bear both an utter sobriety—a soberness—and an ecstatic celebration. Both come from this claim in this moment. Here's the claim:

If we don't succeed in crossing over, we will go extinct.

We're in a new moment in history that we've never been in before. We've never been in anything even vaguely close to this point.

WE HAVEN'T SOLVED THE ISSUES THAT CAUSED CIVILIZATIONS TO FALL—AND WE HAVE A GLOBAL CIVILIZATION

Every single civilization that's risen has fallen. Read Joseph Tainter, *The Collapse of Complex Societies*, 1990. There's no civilization that's risen that hasn't fallen. We now have a global civilization—with exponential technology which causes exponential destruction. This technology is fundamentally not in the hands of responsible states; it is now available to rogue non-state actors around the world. We have exponential technology.

Then we have exponential, emergent, possible scarcity: we're undermining the substrate—meaning the basis of the biosphere in which we live.

- All civilizations fell. We haven't solved any of those problems.
- We now have exponential technology which causes exponential damage.
- And we now have a global civilization.

There's no reason to expect, based on the best readings, that our global civilization will not fall.

My friend Michael Dowd, who just died, wrote a book called *Thank God for Evolution*. It's a great book. Michael Dowd was the great optimist in 2010 when I met him. And he spent the last six years of his life as one of the leaders of what's called *the doomer* community[1]—who are some of the smartest people in the world, who actually didn't look away.

Existential risk is not a hobby. They actually look directly towards it and crunch the numbers and do the statistics. They place their attention on the inner structures. **And they basically have come to the conclusion:** *we're gone.*

William R. Catton wrote a book called *Overshoot: The Ecological Basis of Revolutionary Change*, which is kind of the bible of that community. And there are people like Joanna Macy—the best, brightest, most beautiful minds in the world—who have placed all of their attention on existential risk. They have all come to the same conclusion: *game over. So let's start grieving the death and emerge from the delusion that anything else can happen.*

I don't think that's right. But it's a very powerful position. And it's based on the hard facts. If we lived in a materialist world—meaning a world that was purely material—they would be hardcore right.

THE POSSIBILITY OF THE CROSSING

But they ignored the possibility of the crossing.

And this is deep… It's the notion that **something can emerge:**

- A new fundamental structure of society.

---

1 Doomers are people who are extremely pessimistic or fatalistic about global problems such as overpopulation, peak oil, climate change, ecological overshoot, pollution, nuclear weapons, and runaway artificial intelligence.

- A structure of mind.
- A structure of heart.
- A structure of intimate communion.
- A new way of being.
- A world in which everyone is *all in for all life.*

Can you feel that? Feel a world in which everyone is *all in for all life.*

Where something fundamentally shifts, so do the simple *First Principles* that run life.

Now, you might say *that's starry-eyed, unrealistic, absurd, and ridiculous; let's go home.* But you'd be an idiot if you said that.

Because **the only thing that never changes is that it always changes.**

The Reality of history is that it moves—it shifts.

So it's not that *we're trying to shift this boulder that won't move.* It's that there are shifts and currents and movements.

And we're going to go surfing.

Imagine surfing: we're going to surf. We're going to try and see if we can get into the source code of the whole thing and evolve the source code of consciousness and culture. And we're going to actually effect a crossing.

Again, you still might say *that's absurd.* And a bunch of people are thinking *that it is absurd.* I get that. But stay with me a little bit. **It has actually happened before.**

THE DA VINCI OF TODAY IS THE NEW HUMAN AND THE NEW HUMANITY

The Black Death was sweeping Europe. The pandemic was brutalizing the continent. We're in Florence. Ten families are worried about the papal states and about what's happening, but they said *it can't change.* But then, there's one little group of people who say—

No, no, no. It's a time between worlds. It's a time between stories.

There's a new possibility. There's the possibility of a crossing.

And instead of the *doomer* response, the *denial* response, or the *domination* response (high-tech elites: *let's dominate*), **there's a fourth possibility, which is *a new dawn.*** A new da Vinci emerges. And that da Vinci is not one person, it's a *new human and new humanity.*

If *The Crossing* was just about a successful event or a good book, it wasn't really worth your time. It wasn't worth all of the investment and resource—although we'll have a lovely time together. That's not what we're here to do.

We're here not to teach but *to be.*

- We want to *be* this crossing.
- We want to *be Homo amor.*
- We need to do it with our minds and with our bodies, and we need to incarnate the new possibility.
- **We need to become the new story**. I don't just *tell* the new story—I become the new story. It happens as we're moving through our lives. It happens in the casual conversations. It's happening everywhere.

When we become the new story, something shifts in the very source code of everything.

ARE WE WILLING TO PARTICIPATE TOGETHER IN THE CROSSING?

If I can just ask you just a tender question.

Are we willing to play a larger game?

We're not in self-transformation, we're not in self-development, we're not in *what does this do for me?*

Are we willing to play a larger game? Are we willing to participate in the evolution of love?

We're in Florence. We're da Vinci. It depends on us. It's not some other place somewhere else in the world where it's happening. Believe me, I've searched the world. The other rooms are not happening. You think there's some place else where it's happening and that *you reading this book is just a side event and you can't quite believe that this could matter that much.*

Do you get that? It is hard to believe.

Could this matter that much? That is crazy. **But it does.**

- So are we willing to play a larger game?
- Are we willing to participate together in the evolution of love?
- Are we willing to participate together in *the crossing?*

So here we go. This is *The Crossing.*

CHAPTER TWO

A FIRST-PERSON EXPERIENCE OF EXISTENTIAL RISK

In order to do *the Crossing*, we have to have a first-person experience of existential risk. We're not only going to talk about it in third person and describe the structural and economic generator functions, and the root causes of those functions, of existential risk—although that is all important, and we will get to that.

First we are going to move from third-person to first-person experience. We're going to have our own first-person experience of existential risk—because we're in the Crossing.

We want to reach the optimum point of discomfort where we *feel* the fundamental lack of safety. Only from there can we begin the discussion.

YUVAL HARARI REFLECTS MAINSTREAM CULTURE WHEN HE DECONSTRUCTS MEANING

So let's take a look at a transcript excerpt from a TED Talk by Yuval Harari.

> Many, maybe most legal systems are based on this idea, this belief in human rights.

> But human rights are like heaven and like God. It's just a fictional story that we've invented and spread around.

It may be a very nice story. It may be a very attractive story. We want to believe it. But it's just a story. It's not reality. It's not biological reality.

Just as jellyfish... jellyfish and woodpeckers and ostriches have no rights.

Homo sapiens have no rights, also.

Take a human, cut him open, look inside, you find their blood and you find their heart and lungs and kidneys, but you don't find any rights.

The only place you find rights is in fictional stories that humans have invented and spread around.

The same thing is also true in the political field. States and nations are also like human rights and like God and like heaven. They too are just stories.

A mountain is a Reality. You can see it, you can touch it, you can even smell it.

But Israel or the United States: they are just stories—powerful stories, stories we might want to believe very much. But they are just stories. You cannot really see the United States, you cannot touch it, you cannot smell it.[2]

That is one of the most confusing statements I've ever seen.

It was written by a nice man; I like Yuval. There's a kind of web, ad hominem attack on Yuval, with all manner of conspiracy theories. But we're saying this not to demonize Yuval; he is a very nice and good man. Let's just start there. And Yuval is a very good raconteur and storyteller. He gave great lectures at Hebrew U for several years.

This is one of the most confusing statements you can imagine, containing about four sentences that are correct yet utterly confusing.

---

2 Yuval Noah Harari, "Bananas in Heaven," TEDTalk at TEDxJaffa.

I wouldn't bother bringing this up if Yuval was just speaking as a philosopher. But Yuval is not a philosopher; he is a populist historian. The reason this matters is that **he serves as an unconscious parrot of the primary legacy position of mainstream culture in both open and closed societies**—in an open society like the United States or Europe, and in a closed society like China and other places around the world.

In Yuval's book, *Sapiens*, just as an example, you have Barack Obama saying *it's great—Yuval has got this.* Then there's Bill Gates telling us *he has got it right,* followed by Jeff Bezos, who also claims *he is right.* I could go down a list of 40 other people who endorse the position that *human rights are a complete fantasy, that it's complete fiction—not rooted in anything and without reality. And the only thing that's real is the material world.*

This is a classic expression of materialism which disqualifies the realness of interiors.

Again, it would be utterly uninteresting for me to bring to you if Yuval was just some philosopher. But actually, his position is an unconscious expression of the mainstream legacy position—*which is then offered as science.*

HARARI: "FROM A PURELY SCIENTIFIC VIEWPOINT, HUMAN LIFE HAS ABSOLUTELY NO MEANING"

Harari says, *As far as we can tell from a purely scientific viewpoint, human life has absolutely no meaning.*[3]

Yuval just made up "a purely scientific viewpoint." I've rarely seen that level of intellectual dishonesty and brazenness—because science doesn't talk about this.

So he hijacks science by saying, *this is the scientific viewpoint.*

Human life has absolutely no meaning.

---

3 Yuval Harari, *Sapiens*, Chapter 19, "And They Lived Happily Ever After."

This book *Sapiens* has sold 14 million copies and was endorsed by many. So I'm bringing this as an example of the implicit position. This is the postmodern position that Putin's circle of advisors read—they're not reading Dostoevsky; they don't take Dostoevsky as their source, they're reading postmodern works—that Xi's circle of advisors are reading, which tech titans around the world are reading. **The entire *tech plex*[4] is based on this notion that interiors are not real and that humans are the outcome of blind processes that operate without goals or purpose.**

Harari continues:

> *As far as we can tell from a purely scientific viewpoint, human life has absolutely no meaning. Humans are the outcome of blind evolutionary processes that operate without goal or purpose. Our actions are not part of some divine cosmic plan, and if planet Earth were to blow up tomorrow morning, the universe would probably keep going about its business as usual.*
>
> *As far as we can tell at this point, human subjectivity would not be missed.* ***Hence, any meaning that people inscribe to their lives is just a delusion.***[5]

That flies in the face of the best reads of science—whether that's David Deutsch or Christof Koch or Stuart Kaufman or even Ray Kurzweil, and

---

4   By tech plex, we mean the technological infrastructure of society, which includes the entire planetary stack (Benjamin Bratton's term), as well as the daily immersive environment constituted by social media and the Internet of Things. The tech plex is unique in that it has facilitated a new world in which technology is no longer a tool, but an immersive environment. We live inside of that plex. That plex moves all the way up and all the way down the planetary stack. The tech plex is constituted by infrastructure, social structure, and superstructure, as we have previously defined these terms. Clearly, there's infrastructure, in terms of the actual physical structures of the tech plex. There's social structure, in relationship to the laws that govern and the absence of laws in relationship to the tech plex. And third, there's superstructure. That is to say, the technology actually codifies particular values and ignores or bypasses or rejects other values. That is to say, the tech plex is not value-neutral; the tech plex implies a set of worldviews or superstructures. See David J. Temple, *Invisible Architects: Skinner, Pentland & the Hidden Blueprints for TechnoFeudalism—Exit the Silicon Maze* (forthcoming).
5 Harari, *Sapiens*, Chapter 19, "And They Lived Happily Ever After."

the list goes on. But that's not my point. My point is to get the brazenness of the position. The position is: *Value is not real, it is contrived.*

And **there is a direct path from the notion that *value is not real* to the structures that bring us to existential risk.**

We will deepen what that exact path is—but it's a direct path.

THE FIRST SHOCK OF EXISTENCE IS THE DEATH OF THE INDIVIDUAL HUMAN

In CosmoErotic Humanism[6] we make a distinction between what we call **the first shock of existence and the second shock of existence.**

Just feel into the word "shock." Shock is a disruption. It's sudden. Shock is when *it's not as I thought.*

But the nature of a shock is actually that it builds gradually until it discloses itself.

Often in a relationship, there's a moment when things erupt—but it didn't really erupt over that single moment. It wasn't about *who did this or who didn't do that.* It's about some other set of things that have been happening

---

6   CosmoErotic Humanism is a philosophical movement aimed at reconstructing the collapse of value at the core of global culture. This movement emerges in response to the meta-crisis, understanding existential and catastrophic risks as rooted not only in failures of economics, politics, and technology, but in failed worldviews. The core of CosmoErotic Humanism offers a system of First Principles and First Values that recasts cosmic evolution as a Story of Value in which humanity plays a unique role. These First Principles and First Values ground a comprehensive set of theories, including self and psychology, epistemology, scientific metaphysics, education, theology, mysticism, sexuality, and value. CosmoErotic Humanism thereby responds to the three great questions: *Where? Who?* and *What?* It offers a new Universe story (*Where am I?*), a new narrative of identity (*Who am I?*), and new vision of ethics (*What ought I/we do?*). These are some of the first words on the possibilities of a world philosophy adequate to our time of civilization transformation. What is offered by CosmoErotic Humanism is a new story of *eternal yet evolving* value that can serve as a context for our diversity, finally allowing us to speak of humanity as part of a shared story of evolving cosmic value. See David J. Temple, *First Principles and First Values: Forty-Two Propositions on CosmoErotic Humanism, the Meta-Crisis, and the World to Come* (2024)

over a period of time that only erupted at a particular moment. That's a *shock.*

So, the first shock of existence is at the dawn of human civilization, when *Homo sapiens* begins. We emerge from *Homo erectus,* we emerge from *Homo neanderthalensis*—there are a number of other *Homo* families. And at some point, *Homo sapien*s emerges. We won't go through the arguments in anthropology now.

But there's this moment where *Homo sapiens* emerges. It's very early. As David Graeber, a great historian who passed away recently, pointed out, *Homo sapiens* emerges way before farming. It's really early when the human being becomes human, and he faces, she faces the reality: *I'm going to die.* It's more like, *Fuck, I'm going to die*—if I can get the early citation.

That is the first shock of existence, which is the realization of the death of the individual human being.

We're not going to talk about the continuity of consciousness and what is beyond death right now. I think it's correct that *death is a night between two days.* There is an enormous amount of empirical evidence to suggest so. And we should do an advanced Crossing on death and whatever happens the next day, or the next minute, or the next second after we die. What we wouldn't give to have just five minutes with a loved one that passed. That's a great conversation to have, but it's not our conversation right now.

Death looms in our Reality. And for *Homo sapiens,* death is a cold, sharp end. That's the first shock of existence.

And this first shock of existence *presses us into life.* The realization of the death of the human being *presses us into life.* That's what poet Rainer Maria Rilke writes about[7]—when you read Rilke, he talks about death.

---

7   "The weight of this unexplained and perhaps greatest event, which only due to a misunderstanding has gained the reputation of being arbitrary and cruel, presses us (I think increasingly) more evenly and more deeply into life and places the utmost obligations on our slowly growing strengths." Rainer Maria Rilke, *The Dark Interval: Letters on Loss, Grief, and Transformation* (2018)

Death presses us into life and we go inside and we disclose gnosis—knowing—about Reality.

And all of the worst, but also all of the best of human civilization emerges in response to the first shock of existence. The novel *The Picture of Dorian Gray*, by Oscar Wilde, is about the tragedy of not realizing my death and the decadence that emerges from it. When I actually face my death, I'm born in some profound way.

So the first shock of existence is the realization of the death of the human being.

THE SECOND SHOCK OF EXISTENCE IS THE POTENTIAL DEATH OF HUMANITY

Then we go through all of history—we could go through ten stages of human history—and then we come to the modern period and into post-modernity. All of a sudden, we realize with this jolt: the second shock of existence.

The second shock of existence is not the death of the individual human being, but the imminent potential—and without an intervention, the likely—death of humanity.

The potential death of humanity is the second shock of existence.

Now, if that death were to be realized, it would mean that **all of the past—** which passed onto us all of its hopes, all of its yearnings, all of its dreams, and all of its visions for us to complete, to pick up, to carry on—**would come to naught,** or, in the best scenario, at least the overwhelming majority. See for example Toby Ord's book called *Existential Risk*,[8] where he goes through the details quite intensely. Or Nick Bostrom's *Superintelligence*.[9]

---

8 Toby Ord, *Existential Risk* (Cambridge University Press, 2020).
9 Nick Bostrom, *Superintelligence* (Oxford, 2016).

All the present disappears. Virtually everything disappears—all the past, all the present.

But here's where it gets completely unimaginable.

All of the future disappears.

Everything has come to this generation. For a series of reasons, this is a unique generation in which *global civilization plus exponential technology plus rivalrous conflict, with no Story of Value, equals dead end—extinct, end game, existential risk.*

That's the equation.

We'll discuss that more later, but for now, let's just understand what that means. It means that:

- Trillions of unborn people never live.
- Trillions of love stories never happen.
- Trillions of babies are never healthy.
- Trillions of children are never able to held in the arms of their mother.

An unimaginable gnosis and depth, creativity, goodness, truth, and beauty is stillborn; it's never born into the world.

AS HOMO AMOR WE EMBRACE THE FUTURE GENERATIONS

Literally, the only voice of all the future generations is us.

That's an empirical fact.

In other words, they are not here, they have no vote. The only people who can stand for future generations are the small number of people who step into a new Reality and incorporate into their own consciousness both a deep relationship to the past and an embrace of the fullness of the present,

but particularly—and that's the first demarcating characteristic of *Homo amor*—**they actually embrace and hold in their heart the future.**

That's not easy to do. It's hard for us to hold people who are on the other side of the globe because they're not real to us. So if they're not in our geography, they're hard to hold.

So imagine when they're not only not in our geography, in our *space*, but they're also not in our temporality, in our *time*.

They are the trillions of unborn people. Where are they? They don't exist yet.

So how do we hold them?

- *Homo amor* shatters the boundary of time.
- *Homo amor* is in a covenant that transcends past, present, and future.
- *Homo amor* is on the *inside of the inside* in which all of Eternity and all of Being and all of Becoming lives.

And when I go *to the inside of the inside* on the medicine journey of *Homo amor*, I can feel it all and I can see it all and I embrace it all and I am moved to speak and to act and to love for it all.

HOMO AMOR CROSSES TO THE OTHER SIDE

So *can I love that big*? That's the invitation of *Homo amor*.

How big can I love? How deep is my love? Can I find love in a hopeless place?

I can only do that if I can re-understand the nature of who I am—not based on any fundamentalist claims of the old religions and not based on any fundamentalist claim of the New Age variety, but based on the deepest read of the best sets of facts that we have from the exterior and the interior sciences.

Can we retell the story of *where we are, who we are,* and *what's ours to do?*[10]

That's *Homo sapiens* becoming *Homo amor.*

That is The Crossing. That's the *crossing over* .

And when that crossing happens, something happens.

The first person who did the crossing in history was the great father of Islam and of Hebraicism called Ibrahim.

Ibrahim is *the one who crossed over.* The entire world was on one side.

And "one side" also means "past" in Hebrew; they were lost in the past and they kept repeating the patterns of the past.

Ibrahim crossed to the other side. He realized it was a time between worlds and a time between stories, and **he realized he needed to create the future.**

In the interior sciences, it is said **that this movement of a small group of people changed the entire vector of history**. For example, philosopher Paul Tillich said it was only a thousand people altogether in the entire Renaissance who crossed to the other side, that changed the entire vector of history.

THE SECOND SHOCK OF EXISTENCE: THE 2020s: THE PANDEMIC SHOCK

I'm going to ask you to read this next section with a radically open heart.

I'm going to describe the nature of *the second shock* that we are facing as a species right now. Because it doesn't happen at once. It happens gradually.

It started in the 2020s with the pandemic shock. Who would have thought that we would be locked in our houses and unable to leave them at risk of

---

10 These are the three great questions of CosmoErotic Humanism. See David J. Temple , *First Principles and First Values* (2024).

potential death? All of a sudden, class, race and age didn't seem to matter. The skull grinned at the banquet while death reared her head. It was literally the first shock of existence, *my individual death*—but it also represented the potential specter of the second shock of existence, *the potential death of humanity*. For example, consider the potential specter of bioweapons. Did the pandemic start from rats in the Wuhan market? Did it start from gain-of-function research funded by the United States and China together? Was it a misplaced bioweapon? There's enormous of literature on it—but it really doesn't matter; the point is that **"local" disappeared**. Something happened in this remote province in China that instantly spread around the world. Utter confusion reigned. Five million people died. The pandemic shock.

We realized what many of us had been saying for several decades; we all had this direct realization that *it is not too big to fail.*

We think the pandemic ended. But actually, **for hundreds and hundreds of millions of people, life as they knew it actually ended.**

The privileged—and most of the people reading this are likely in that class—we have largely returned to *business as usual*. We prayed for normalization: *let things go back to normal—the pandemic's over.* But for hundreds and hundreds of millions of people who had spent their entire lives saving up to start a business, saving up to get out of poverty, saving up to send their first daughter to school, saving up to stave off starvation and begin to enter a world of dignity—all of that collapsed. Savings were wiped out, generations of work were wiped out—and we're dissociated from it. Hundreds of millions of people around the world today remain devastated. And yet we try and go back as quickly as we can to *business as usual*, trying to somehow put the pandemic shock behind us.

It's the 2020s—and we spend the 2020s consuming and consuming and consuming. **In China, Russia, the United States, and Europe, consumption has become the standard of our health. And we somehow think we can ignore the pandemic.**

We forget that it was but a dress rehearsal.

We forget that the potential of a next wave of pandemics catastrophically outstrips this pandemic—and almost definitely will come.

We keep going on *business as usual.*

David Attenborough, a biologist and respected figure in the U.K., thinks the following timeline I'm about to describe is going to be in forty, or fifty years from now. Another close friend who's an expert in these matters thinks that this timeline I'm about to describe is absurd in that there's not nearly as much time. Then there are others who think it's a hundred years. But many think it's the 2020s, 2030s, 2040s, and 2050s. I'm not here to resolve that issue. It doesn't really matter.

Is it the next forty or fifty years? Is it us or is it our children? It doesn't really matter. **What matters is that it's happening.**

So I'm going to describe it. We described the 2020s as the pandemic shock. We will describe the 2030s as the **climate shock**.

THE SECOND SHOCK OF EXISTENCE: THE 2030s: THE CLIMATE SHOCK

So now I want to move to the 2030s. We think we've gotten over the pandemic shock—and then we're hit by the next level of shock, and that is climate shock. It's not a one-time shock, but just like everything we're going to describe here, it's an incremental, step-by-step process.

We gradually get used to it day by day until one day, it all comes together—and we wake up to the full impact of all the separate events and are devastated by the full extent of the shock. Just like the pandemic shock, the climate shock moves in waves, appearing and disappearing, thundering and whispering.

> *In the 2030s, the climate collapse predicted by virtually all of science will explode into our daily lives.*

What does this look like? Remember that in much of the world, most human beings—the United States is just one example of many countries— are actually living paycheck to paycheck, dying in debt with no tangible assets. At the end of the 2020s, for these people, it seems like it can't get much worse.

But then the effects of climate shock enter the picture.

To really understand what that means, let's just look at the economic impact on the average family's ability to put food on the table or a roof over their heads. So right now, you pay something like a quarter of your income for utilities—water about 5%, electricity another 5%, insurance another 5%, and so forth.

Fast forward a decade, and the world is now running out of water, clean air, or livable temperatures. Guess which bills suddenly spike? Your water bill now comes to 20% of your income. Your electricity bill increases because you've got to run extra AC now, night and day, which comes to another 20%. *Bang*, there goes your life. You're already in perpetual, unpayable debt. **What's going to happen when the costs of the climate crisis land squarely on your shoulders?**

Then, one day, you get a bill from the insurance company. Your home insurance premium is going to go up 50% a year because of the risk of fire, flood, or quake. You feel a sudden surge of panic.

Your income has been stuck for most of your life. All your credit cards are perpetually maxed out. How can you afford this? What do you do?

So in the 2020s, my friends—mega-fires and mega-floods, does that sound familiar to anyone?—mega-fires and mega-floods continue to rage out of control, but we don't really notice them. They're a headline one day; they're gone the next. Sea levels rise, lands burn.

Burning and flooding of houses and neighborhoods, residential and industrial, become regular events on the news—and we barely notice.

The 2030s, that accelerates even more and makes entire areas uninhabitable.

- In the 2020s, people were in lockdown. They couldn't leave their homes.
- In the 2030s, huge swaths of people will actually lose their homes to fires and floods.

In the 2020s, the coronavirus and its direct and indirect impacts caused people to lose their jobs. Many people gave up. For those who didn't, all of their energy was poured into the desperate struggle to retrain, redirect, and find new jobs. However, **by the 2030s, there will simply be no jobs to be had.**

Entire geographic areas, from neighborhoods to cities, and even regions, are forced to close down due to flooding resulting from rising tides and fires.

- During the 2020s, societies came to a complete standstill. Governments had to step in and artificially fix the broken economies.
- In the 2030s, governments no longer will have the capacity to bail out economies.

Indeed, economies as we know them effectively cease to exist. Why? Because banks, insurance companies, and mutual funds see their holdings plunge in value. Many, if not most, go bankrupt. The savings of large sectors of society are burned and washed away.

This, in turn, causes waves of small businesses to shut down, and this, in turn, generates a massive next wave of unemployment.

Dry cleaners close; those chemicals are now too toxic to afford.

Brewers and butcheries shut their doors. Who could afford meat anymore?

Who can afford water spent for pleasure when it was needed to quell the raging fires?

Shops? Who was going to insure them?

Rent spirals out of control.

No kind of business is left unaffected.

Industrial capitalist civilization can no longer employ people.

The world is now too precarious to live on. Incomes have collapsed. And who knows how to make ends meet?

- In the 2020s, people survived the coronavirus depression by taking on debts and selling their assets: homes, savings, bonds, and retirement funds.
- In the 2030s, not only are there few of those left, but there are no real buyers who wanted to buy your home or give you credit.

The financial system can't cope with the risks of climate change to begin with. Insurance companies go bankrupt, taking banks and funds down with them, causing individuals' remaining savings and investments to collapse. Even worse, there is no one to turn to for credit, debt, insurance, or adequate employment.

Cash is the only thing worth having—if you could even get any. There's no one to guarantee credit—which has become a survival need. You can't survive without credit, particularly as prices spiral out of control because of the sudden scarcity of supply. The average person has no access to any sort of working capital.

And the chasm, the huge gap between the elites and the rest of the world, widens to a breaking point. The old Indian caste system seems a joke by comparison to what emerges.

That's the climate shock of the 2030s.

- People's lives collapse.
- Basic human needs, which were a titanic struggle in the 2020s, have now become impossible to afford. By basic needs, we mean education, housing and healthcare.
- The old notion of a workplace has all but disappeared.
- Human identity is completely confused. Without jobs, there's no value (we've all read Yuval Harari's quote above on how human life has no meaning).

Then depression overtakes reality—because the nature of depression is futility: *there's no purpose, there's no plot line.*

A radical sense of powerless poison permeates human hearts.

What happens is most people turn to *gig work*—you hop from job to job. As climate shock tears the backbone of economies apart, people become more like nomads—job-hopping, traveling market traders like from a thousand years ago. Middle-class folks with stable, simple jobs disappear.

Fixed salaries disappear. One day you get a little work in this city, the next day you get a little work in the next city. You hop jobs and hop jobs and hop jobs.

And all of this is just the beginning of a description of climate shock.

Kids going to school need clean air, water, food, and energy—but in the 2030s all those things are in short supply. Who can afford to run a world-class school when prices of those basics have spiraled out of control? Your kids can go to school *some* days, but it's a charade.

The government is a charade.

Voting is a charade.

Google and Facebook are all super strong, monitoring every move and shaping your desires as you're plugged into the internet 24 hours a day because the actual world isn't engageable.

Schools require clean air, water, and food, which are not quite available. Similarly, hospitals depend on a consistent supply of medicine, energy, sanitation, and hygiene—but all those things seem to be vanishing (there are brownouts *nowadays* when water just stops flowing).

There are days when the smog is so bad you can barely leave the house. You can go to the hospital, sure, but like school, it is barely functional; a decrepit place, a broken system. You're probably better off at home taking your chances.

THE SECOND SHOCK OF EXISTENCE: THE 2040s: THE EXTINCTION SHOCK

Then we move from the climate shock of the 2030s to the extinction shock of the 2040s.

- ◆ 2020s: pandemic shock.
- ◆ 2030s: climate shock.
- ◆ 2040s: extinction shock.

In the 2040s, we come to this explosion, which is the sixth mass extinction[11] itself, when we begin to exterminate the very substrate of the biosphere on which our own lives depend. And as always, the most vulnerable, with no voice to speak for themselves, are the first victims. Forms of insects, coral reefs, butterflies, and bees—all sentient, magical living beings, and beings upon whom we depend for life—go extinct first.

---

11 The sixth mass extinction refers to the ongoing, human-driven loss of biodiversity on Earth, with species disappearing at rates far higher than the natural background rate. It follows five previous mass extinction events in Earth's history, the last of which wiped out the dinosaurs.

But **we barely notice because we can't even pay attention, we're so in pain.**

Then they're followed by entire groups of fish, birds, mammals, reptiles, and trees. Those sentient beings that have been the basis of the great ecological change—are going extinct.

Read and listen carefully, my friends, from the heart, on the inside.

The foundation of the Earth system is ripped away. Naturally, the great ecological edifices upon which they are built collapse. Remember, it's the fish that clean our rivers. It's the insects that turn our soil, which grow our crops. **What happens when we have no river water we can drink and no crops that take root because there's no healthy soil?**

Imagine the 2040s, as temperatures continue to rise, water and food grow scarcer, and oxygen levels decline due to the loss of trees. Entire ecosystems start to collapse and tip over.

- A vast forest dies and turns into a desert.
- A river turns dank and muddy.
- A series of lakes suddenly seems to turn poisonous.
- The oceans empties one day and is full of strange invaders the next.
- The topsoil itself turns to poison.

Nature itself seems to have gone insane. Every month brings a fresh nightmare and a new surprise. What ecologists have described in great detail all along is now happening. However, there's barely anyone who has the energy to struggle to understand it. The ecosystems are toppling over like great and vast towers whose foundations have been ripped away. The stability of the seasons as we know them is finally disappearing for good.

Extinction shock builds upon climate shock and pandemic shock, adding devastating dimensions to food chains, water tables, and raw materials. The very structure of life is now ripped away.

A harvest fails, followed by another. The cost of everything from wheat to tea to bread explodes. And then, my friends, we begin to reach the 2050s.

The world has now exploded. The collapse of identity gives rise to a dark tide of rage. The realization begins to dawn that the whole thing is failing. But there is a far more horrific quality that poisons Reality. It's the dead-end stupor, the zombification of extinction shock in which huge masses of the world's population—billions upon billions of people—realize that **there is no North Star of value to follow.**

No new Stories of Value[12] were articulated. The resources were not allocated.

Exterior sciences exploded while the interior sciences[13] ground to a halt; we evolved all of our technology-driven profit mechanisms but the interior sciences came to a stop. **There's no new Story of Value to take us home.**

The tech elites, cloistered away, continue to prosper. A wave of violence spreads across the globe.

Think of the movie *Mad Max*, where resources are suddenly in desperately short supply. Poverty inevitably leads to extreme violence, like it always does.

THE SECOND SHOCK OF EXISTENCE: THE 2050s: THE SHOCK OF CIVILIZATIONAL COLLAPSE

Then we get to the shock of *civilizational collapse* in the 2050s.

This is the 2050s. The end game of civilization begins in earnest. Societies turn against one another, within and without. States declare independence.

---

12 By new "Story of Value" we mean that story is ontological, fundamental to the Cosmos in which we participate. Story is always a Story of Value, characterized by intrinsic movements of meaning, consciousness, and information. See chapter 11 of David. J. Temple, *First Principles and First Values* (2024).

13 By "interior sciences," we mean the investigation of reality from a philosophical, spiritual, or religious perspective.

It's a war of all against all. Each military is busy fighting wars for water, air, medicine, food, and labor.

In Europe, nations attempt to defend themselves against Russia, which is now a violent aggressor seeking to seize resources. Unfortunately, they mostly fail.

In Asia, China bought its own form of order. *The Belt and Road Initiative*[14] now reveals its true face. Asia and large parts of Africa are completely controlled by China. China rules brutally to feed and clothe its homeland.

In the 2040s shock of extinction, authoritarianism and doomsday cults ruled. Concentration camps ramped up the abuse of immigrants. Local massacres were commonplace because *who had the energy to stop them*? But in the 2050s, in a world where the rivers were running dry and the oceans were turning to dust, *wasn't it only fair to blame all that misery on the dirty, filthy sub-humans who had caused it*? So **the worst kinds of racism and hatred explode** as food chains implode, as water tables become salt, as medicine can no longer be made because the raw ingredients are not accessible. **There are no more elemental resources to be mined without a working system.**

There is no insulin, antibiotics, milk, eggs, bread, vegetables, computers, cars, or furniture—all those disappear because they can't exist without the ecosystems that supply air, wood, water, and metal.

Somewhere over these decades, or whatever time period it takes for each of these stages to unfold, **flourishing civilization as we know it ends.**

With this, you feel a sense of bitter disappointment: *It wasn't supposed to be like this.* You try and calm yourself after a moment of seeing red. After all, you're smart enough to see the effects.

---

14 The Belt and Road Initiative (BRI) is a global infrastructure and investment strategy launched by China in 2013 to enhance trade and economic connectivity across Asia, Africa, and Europe through a network of railways, ports, highways, and other projects.

Living on the edge of despair has led to massive waves of people seemingly losing their minds. They cling to bizarre superstitions, spend all day in escapism, flee to conspiracy theories, or, worst of all, join many of the new doomsday cults flourishing everywhere. But in the end, it all slowly grinds to a halt.

There you were, an average person trapped in a vicious cycle of self-preservation—too poor, too weary, too tired, and too broken to do anything but watch in panic, fear, and fury as a new dark age emerged and one by one the lights of civilization went out.

This is not a fantasy.

It's been described again and again.

First, it was described in the literature of science fiction, and then since 1960, and then into the 70s, and into the 80s, and into the 90s. It's been carefully, meticulously researched and documented.

Whatever the exact timeline is, right now **this is the virtually inevitable course of events.**

My friend Michael Dowd, who wrote the book *Thank God for Evolution*, was one of the great optimists of the last twenty years. He recently passed away. He said to me, "In the end, I need to move from denial and actually embrace the doom." He said, "Sometimes it breaks my heart, but mostly I just live with the sense that I've been given a terminal diagnosis. I'm committed to living fully, loving my life, being a blessing to others, and making a contribution to my neighbors. But yeah, I don't think my granddaughter will reach the age of 20. I don't think she'll even reach the age of 10. But I'm committed that she has the best life possible, as long as possible." And Michael represents one of the best researchers in the world.

He's joined by dozens of the clearest thinkers who have embraced the *doomer* position and view the collapse of hope and the beginning of the grieving as the only possible honest response to Reality.

To blithely say *they're wrong* is moral bankruptcy combined with moral idiocy—which is a bad combination.

So how do we respond?

We respond with *The Crossing*. And that's what this book is about.

WE CAN ROW THE BOAT ASHORE, *HALLELUJAH*

Let's close for now with a song that comes from the neighborhood I grew up in, in Columbus, Ohio, where people still had porches and you could kind of hang out in the street.

My street was particularly non-religious, it was a very secular street, and everyone took pride in having nothing to do with churches or synagogues. However, there was a song that people sang because it was an integral part of the fabric of Reality.

Now, I haven't actually heard the song until the other night. I just happened to hear it. And I was like, *Wow, I remember that song.*

Now, we can't *go back* to that song. But we can actually *go forward* to the song.

And it goes like this:

> *Michael, row the boat ashore, Hallelujah*
>
> *Michael, row the boat ashore, Hallelujah*
>
> *Sister, help to trim the sails (Hallelujah)*
>
> *Sister, help to trim the sails (Hallelujah)*
>
> *(Michael, row the boat ashore, Hallelujah*
>
> *Michael, row the boat ashore, Hallelujah)*
>
> *The River Jordan is chilly and cold (Hallelujah)*
>
> *Chills the body but not the soul (Hallelujah)*

Michael, row the boat ashore, Hallelujah

Michael, row the boat ashore, Hallelujah

River is deep, and the river is wide (Hallelujah)

Milk and honey on the other side (Hallelujah)

Michael, row the boat ashore, Hallelujah.

Michael, row the boat ashore, Hallelujah. [15]

See if you can find inside yourself, not an override, but a place inside that knows that **after you've heard everything, there actually is hope.**

That's what this song is about. See if you can find that place. And maybe you'll put the song on wherever you are and sing it. But don't sing it as a campfire song. It's not a public performance; it's not girl scouts. It's a subtle practice.

After all of that, there is great hope.

See if you can find that.

It's like, *Oh, we can row the boat ashore.*

And then, we hold silence, which is not a silence of absence, but *a silence of presence.*

---

15 Lyrics of the song "Michael" by the Highwaymen.

CHAPTER THREE

HOMO AMOR INJUNCTION ONE: LET YOUR HEART BE BROKEN

THERE IS NOTHING MORE WHOLE THAN A BROKEN HEART

We're going to step into the eight injunctions—eight stages on the journey of becoming *Homo amor*.

The first injunction is: *let your heart be broken*.

And maybe we could add to it: *there's nothing more whole than a broken heart*.

So that's the injunction we're in.

Let your heart be broken; there is nothing more whole than a broken heart.

PRAYER: "I DON'T BELIEVE IN GOD, BUT I BELIEVE IN PRAYER"

Let's first spend a moment on prayer.

My friend Warren Farrell, who some of you know, must be about 80 years old. He was with Gloria Steinem, one of the leaders of the emergence of men's and women's movements in the United States. Warren grew up with a certain caricature of a certain god-in-the-sky. He grew up with his mother chasing him around the house angrily. To say it lightly, she was not attuned. He would run into the bathroom and his mother would bang on the door and say, *god's going to get you in there.* So God and Warren didn't do well.

But of course, the god you don't believe in, I don't believe in either. The god you don't believe in doesn't exist. There's a holy heresy. Yuval Harari, whose text we looked at before, is not entirely wrong. He's dismissing something important. He's rejecting something important. I'm with him in that rejection. He's rejecting an old caricatured version of god whose excessive focus is your pattern of masturbation. *Wow!* Not that god. Not the god who says, *these are the chosen people, and these people are unchosen.* Not that god. That's what we mean when we say, *the god you don't believe in, doesn't exist.* As we got to know each other, Warren would always say to me, "I can't really have that conversation with you. But what I'll grant you is: *I don't believe in God, but I believe in prayer.*" So let's start there.

PRAYER: AN EXPRESSION OF OUR INCONSOLABLY DEEP YEARNING

Prayer is the knowing that I'm yearning for something. Now, imagine I had a conversation with a fish. You would never hear a fish say, *I am yearning for dry land. If only I could find some dry land.* No, because fish don't yearn for dry land. It's not in their nature. It's not the field they participate in.

We have an inconsolable longing, a deep yearning—across culture, space, and time—for a journey of transformation. We reach for something wider. *We want to know what love is.* And that is of overwhelming, overriding, unimaginable importance to us. We give up everything for it.

How many people have had that experience where you're in this exchange with someone, and it's a love exchange, and they haven't texted you back? You're sitting there by your phone. And your business deals fall to the side.

And everything you're doing disappears. All you're doing is waiting. And then… you see *dot, dot, dot…* your beloved typing a message back.

We want to know what love is. But we already know it! It lives inside of us.

That is our prayer today. *I want to know what love is.* Let's pray it together. The song "I Want to Know What Love Is" by *The Foreigner* is our prayer anthem. If you can, turn it on now and pray along!

I want to know what love is, I want you to show me. Homo amor.

In your heart, body, mind, let's turn to *Homo amor* within and say:

- I am *Homo amor.*
- I shift my orientation to Reality.
- I'm tender and fierce.
- I take responsibility for the whole.

And we ask ourselves: **How can I, in this moment, in this day, be Homo amor?** How can we be *Homo amor* today? And how can we take responsibility for the whole right now?

HOMO AMOR IS WILLING TO LET HER HEART BE BROKEN OPEN

The injunction is to let your heart be broken. Our intention is to become *Homo amor.* We invoke *Homo amor.* And one of the qualities of *Homo amor* is that *Homo amor* is willing to let his or her heart be broken.

Homo amor is willing to let his or her heart be broken—and not only in the realm of the personal, which is related to the details of my beautiful, important personal life.

- Homo amor is willing to open her heart, his heart, and let it be broken by people who live across the world.

33

- *Homo amor* is willing to open her heart, his heart, to people that live in the future.

***Homo amor* holds the past, holds the present, and holds the future.**

WE MUST DEMOCRATIZE HOMO AMOR

There has always been *Homo amor*. There's always a little *Homo amor* in every *Homo sapiens*. That's why *Homo amor* is the fulfillment of *Homo sapiens*. It's not a sharp break.

And there have always been heroes, and masters, and rishis, and saints who held the past and the present and the future. *Homo amor* has always been present.

And *Homo amor* used to be an elite, but **in order to respond to the meta-crisis** and in order to respond to the deepest yearnings of our own inconsolable longing, **we have to democratize *Homo amor.***

We have to all become *Homo amor.*

It simply won't work to have a group of elites who are holding *Homo amor.*

We have to all literally become *Homo amor.*

There has to be a fundamental evolutionary shift in which Homo amor is born as the default.

A thousand years ago, we said that there should be some concept of democracy in the world, where people would choose who governs them. It was an absurd notion. Yet, at least for two or three hundred years, democracy has lived in the world. It's now dying. It's now becoming more of an illusion and a facade. What actually runs elections, and how they determine governance is complex. **But the notion that democracy could**

exist was absurd a thousand years ago—and then it was born and it became a possibility.

So our intention is both completely for ourselves and completely beyond our individual selves. Yes, we are madly excited that we are all on this unimaginably great personal journey together. But that's an insufficient reason.

Our overwhelming concern is: *we have to become, and we have to model the Crossing.* And we have to get it precisely.

Meaning, *what are the elements needed to cross over?* And if we're missing this—even though it might work in our own personal lives—**if it won't work in the room of Reality, it is insufficient**. Then there's something essentially missing that we skipped.

We can't just dismiss Yuval. We have to understand him. We have to understand what he's emerging from, and what he got right and what he got wrong.

We can't create new polarizations. We have to create higher paradoxes and greater wholeness. A new world of *us-them* won't take us home.

We've got to have a place where it's a world that works for everyone and where everyone has a seat at the table. And from there emerges a new dream, a new vision, a new story, a new possibility.

So what we want to do in this book, is way too much.[16] But it's all essentially necessary. Without any piece of it, it doesn't fly. So, let's go deep.

There's nothing I've taken off the table, thinking, *Oh they won't get it; it'll be too hard, it'll be too complex.* There's nothing that we can't do. So, let's go.

Are we good? Are we awake? Are we alive? Let's do this.

---

16   This book of oral essays on The Crossing is part of an entire Great Library articulating the new Story of Value we are calling CosmoErotic Humanism. See https://worldphilosophyandreligion.org/books/ for more.

THE MOVE FROM PRE-TRAGIC TO TRAGIC TO POST-TRAGIC

Step one—*let your heart be broken.* So, what does that mean? That means that we have to move—in what we call using *Homo amor* language—from the pre-tragic to the tragic to the post-tragic.

What is the nature of the pre-tragic? The nature of the pre-tragic is clarity: *everything is clear. I understand why people suffer. I understand why people die.* That's one version of the pre-tragic. It reflects the pre-modern religion in its shadow, which Yuval Harari is rightfully rebelling against.

That doesn't work.

Pre-tragic means I understand exactly what everyone should do at every moment of the day.

One possibility of the pre-tragic is the notion that the individual is merely an illusion.

Another possibility is that *I'm focused on ensuring that my family's wealth is passed down to the next two generations, just as the last two generations did; I have a family business, and I'm determined to transition it effectively, so it persists for two or three more generations in a different world.*

Pre-tragic also means *the world that I grew up in is the world that's going to exist. It's clear. Its parameters are clear, my vacations are clear, and my vacation destinations are clear. I'm going to live my life the way the last two generations have lived theirs.* That's pre-tragic.

Pre-tragic means *I have clarity, it's worked out, and I won't allow the tragic to intrude on the pre-tragic.*

Does everyone understand that?

There are many ways to play the pre-tragic game. But the point is, one way or another, **I've closed my heart.**

For example, I may have closed my heart because I'm a religious fundamentalist. My brother was a beautiful man who died years ago in a car crash. He was a gorgeous young man with ten kids who lived in Staten Island, New York. Any poor family in Staten Island that needed anything could go to his house 24 hours a day. He was a gorgeous young man. He took over the organizations I ran in the fundamentalist world alongside his wife, Miriam, who used to be my assistant—and who has just passed. The reason they didn't go with me to the next stage is because they wanted clarity. If you were to call Devin and Miriam, and something happened in the world, they would immediately have a set of texts that explained exactly why it happened. *It happened for this reason, in this way, because there's this text, this explanation, and this theological model.*

But actually:

+ *Homo amor* holds certainty and clarity.
+ *Homo amor* holds the mystery.

The god you don't believe in doesn't exist. We reject the pre-tragic notion that says: *My life will continue exactly as it is, and the world will remain unchanged. I will live within a certain level of middle- or upper-middle-class privilege, facing the same set of challenges, and my life will be confined to this narrow personal existence.*

That's simply not going to happen. This is pre-tragic. It is not true. It's a false sense of clarity, where I'm not willing to open up to what's really true.

I have to transition from the pre-tragic to the tragic. That's painful. And when the tragic is existential risk… of course, I look away.

I have to begin to become Homo amor by opening my heart so wide that I can hold existential risk before I even attempt to solve it.

Existential risk is not easily solvable—but I can engage it, I can respond, I can affect its trajectory.

We'll get there, **but first I just have to be willing to be in it, to hold it.**

Sometimes we come closer, sometimes we step back, but we never look away.

Robert Jay Lifton, one of the most important writers of the last generation, wrote about the Nazi doctors in his 1986 book *The Nazi Doctors: Medical Killing and the Psychology of Genocide.* He also contributed an essay to the anthology *Facing Apocalypse,* published in the early 1980s. It is a critical work. It's a definite read. Top of the list.

Facing apocalypse means *I'm willing to not turn away.*

That's the move from the pre-tragic to the tragic.

THE EVOLUTION OF TEARS

Now, let's talk about tears.[17] When a baby is born, the baby cries. That's how we know a baby is healthy. I had the privilege of being at the birth of all four of my children. The baby cries.

The inability to cry is tragic.

But when you can't cry, it's also enough to *want* to cry. Even wanting to cry is crying.

If you want to trace the trajectory of human emergence, you could say that evolution itself is the evolution of tears.

Tears are not static; tears are not just something that happens. Tears are actually an expression of my deepest gnosis.

But I have to cultivate my tears. I have to learn the language of my tears. I have to hear the voice of my tears.

---

17   See Marc Gafni, *Tears* (2005).

What does it mean to be alive? **To be alive is to participate uniquely in the evolution of tears.**

We know that chemically, tears that respond to different circumstances have different interior structures, different exterior structures, and different chemical structures. They don't look the same. If you actually look at an image of tears, it's a dazzling artistic configuration, and they look different in relation to why and how I'm crying. So I need to be in relationship to my tears.

THE SECOND SIMPLICITY OF TEARS

My teacher's teacher is from a little town called Kutz. My teacher actually died about 150 years ago. I never met him—which gives me a little more latitude.

He writes that the young boy cries and says, *Where? Who? What? Why?* And the boy doesn't know. The baby doesn't know. The girl doesn't know.

And then we cry—and we get some answers. Those tears are usually somewhat superficial and somewhat serious. It's a mix.

We go through life, and at each stage, we throw off the answers, we cry again, we take on a new set of answers, and we throw them off again.

So we start with a simple elemental simplicity, and we go to complexity, and then we go to second simplicity, and then we go to more complexity, and then to a next simplicity. Until I become an old man and an old woman, and a wise man, and a wise woman and then I cry again, and what do I say? *What? Where? Who? Why?*

But the tears are fundamentally different. They're completely distinct. I've gone through so many levels. I've gone so deep on the inside of the inside, **and now my tears hold everything**.

WHAT DOES GOD DO ON THE INSIDE OF THE INSIDE?

There's a text that was written in 1944 by a master named Kalonimus Kalman Shapiro of Piacezna. He was in Treblinka, one of the Nazi concentration camps. He'd survived the Warsaw Ghetto Uprising. And he's at the end of his life, clearly. He would write these teachings every week and bury them. He was killed. The teachings were discovered in 1960.

In one of his teachings, he asks the following question—and in this lineage that he comes from, everything is about text. So he says, "There are two verses in the great prophet Jeremiah in response to the following question: What does God do on the inside?"

That's a realization question; that's an erotic, mystical question. **It's not a theological question.** Does everyone get the difference? I want to be *on the inside*. What's happening in Reality on the inside? On the *inside of the inside*, what's happening?

What does God do on the inside?

So he says, "One text says, on the inside, Reality is filled with joy. It's filled with goodness. It's filled with pulsing aliveness. It's not concerned. It's indifferent to the goings on in this world. It's Infinity." That's one text.

The second text is, "On *the inside of the inside*, Reality is crying."

So Kalonimus Kalman says, "The reason that Reality cries on *the inside of the inside* is that **if but one tear fell from the Infinite on the outside, the world would be destroyed.**"

"But," he says, "the master"—*Homo amor*—"is so audacious, is so filled with courage, that she's willing to enter *the inside of the inside* to cry with You."

And in that participation mystique, when I participate, when I hold the whole, and I cry the tears of the whole, it is already healed. It already begins to be healed.

The confusion begins to clarify. The Hebrew word for tears is *bechi*, which means radical confusion.

But when all the gates are closed, the gates of tears are open.

And *Homo amor* cries the tears of the whole.

And that, paradoxically, my friends, is the beginning of the move from the tragic to the post-tragic. See, we don't stay at the tragic.

THERE IS A VISION OF ARMAGEDDON AND OF MESSIAH IN EVERY LINEAGE

How many people have heard of the term *Armageddon*? We've heard the term, right? So, what is Armageddon? In Christian apocalyptic literature, it's a term for some violent convulsion at the end of days, right?

But I'll tell you something wild.

- If you read Theravadan Buddhist literature, you'll find something similar.
- If you read Vajrayana, later in Buddhism, you'll find something similar.
- If you read certain strands of Plato, you'll find something similar.
- If you read Kashmir Shaivism, the root tradition of Hinduism, you'll find something similar.
- If you read Hebrew wisdom, you'll find something similar.

This gives a sense of how every great lineage tradition had a sense that we would come to a moment of rupture. It's kind of wild. They were all describing existential risk, although they didn't have that language.

Not many people have ever combined these different kinds of literature—because people read in very narrow boxes. We have existential risk thinkers, like Nick Bostrom, who presents himself as an avowed atheist, and he's reading all of the structural analyses of Reality, yet it wouldn't occur to him to turn to lineages. And the lineages, of course, are doing their lineage thing, each in its own place, and beautifully so. But actually, every single major world lineage has a vision of existential risk.

And every single major world lineage has a vision of a different possibility. And there are different names for it.

Now, how many people have heard the word *Messiah*? *Messiah* is not *a person riding on a donkey entering Jerusalem*, as it's described. If you actually read the lineage texts across traditions, across space, and across time, *Messiah* is referred to as *Komat Mashiach*, which is the fullest potentiality of the human being in the full flowering of their Value, Eros, and gorgeous Divinity, emerging as a new possibility.

In every single lineage tradition, there is a contrast between the two possibilities. Now, that's not a small deal. That's a big deal. In other words, **existential risk and *Homo amor* is actually coded in the source code of Reality**. And it's this moment that was actually understood in the lineages. It's not that it was predicted by Nostradamus—do you understand that's not what I'm saying? I'm saying that **there was a realization, an intuition across traditions, that there's a certain moment when we come to a fork in the road**. And the question is: are we going to take the road less traveled?

HOMO AMOR IS BACKED BY THE UNIVERSE

The possibility of *Homo amor* actually lives in the very fabric of Reality. Let's shift our focus from lineages to cosmology.

So, there's a first Big Bang in cosmology. And what's the first Big Bang? It's when the unmanifest becomes manifest: out of nothing, no-thing, there's something, and Reality explodes. Reality is filled with value, by the way: mystical value, musical value, mathematical value, scientific value, molecular value, macrobiotic value, moral value…

So Reality explodes—**the first Big Bang.** Are you familiar with that? The first Big Bang, about 13.7 billion years ago—the exact timing is another conversation. But there was a first Big Bang. And what happens after that? We move through the entire unfolding of the world of matter.

But, stay with me:

It's not just a world of "matter." It's a world of "what matters."

It's not just *matter*, the world's coded with value. It's *what matters*.

When a proton gets together with a neutron, 380,000 years after the Big Bang, it's coded with value. There's a unique attraction. There's not just matter—there's what matters. There are gazillions of quarks in the first nanoseconds. But not all quarks can get together. They're actually codes of what matters.

But, let's bracket that for a second.

We go through the first explosion of the Big Bang, and matter, all the stages of matter—billions of years of matter, stage after stage, deeper and deeper expressions, and more and more coherent expressions.

And then, all of matter triumphs, all of the physiosphere triumphs in a second Big Bang. **The second Big Bang is the triumph of matter into life: the physiosphere becomes the biosphere**. You've got this intensification that takes place, and all of a sudden, *voila*, you've got this momentous Big Bang, literally, something from nothing again. We have a biosphere—we have life.

So what happens next? We go from an original cell, from prokaryotes to eukaryotes, from single-cell organisms to multicellular life. Then come the early plants, and we get some fish in there. It goes neural net, neural cord, and it continues upward along the evolutionary chain: early animals, later animals, mammals, hominids. It's this whole evolutionary story, moving through stage after stage after stage of life in the biosphere.

And then what happens? Then there is a third Big Bang, and **all of life triumphs again as the depths of the human self-reflective mind—*Homo sapiens*.** *Wow!*

We've gone from the *physiosphere*, to the *biosphere*, to what the early Russian cosmists in 1915 called the *noosphere*: the world of culture, the world of interior mind. The world of the interior mind becomes awake. The interior mind existed before; there were always interiors, but now there's a deepening of the interior mind, this transmission of information, this explosion of the depth of the human self-reflective mind. That's the third Big Bang.

Let me ask you a question: does it just end there? Game over?

No! The actual understanding of the leading edges, both in the complexity sciences and in the lineages, is that it keeps deepening and deepening and deepening.

- We go from quarks all the way to culture.[18]
- We go from mud to Mozart.
- We go from bacteria to Bach.
- We go from dirt to Dostoevsky.
- We go from slime to Shakespeare.

There's this emergence, there's this pattern, there's this direction, there's this plot line.

And then, *give me a drum roll...*

And then, and then, and then, and then, and then...?

Then there is a possibility for the world of the depth of the self-reflective human mind to triumph into a new emergence.

---

18 See Marc Gafni, *The Evolution of Love from Quarks to Culture* (2025).

Just like matter triumphed as life, and life triumphed as the depth of the self-reflective human mind, there's a new possibility that the depth of the self-reflective human mind, Homo sapiens, triumphs as Homo amor.

So that's a very big deal: when you actually realize that *Homo amor* is backed by the Universe. **Homo amor is backed by the Universe.** It's not an absurd possibility. It's not some frivolous dream. **It's actually the erotic movement of evolution itself.**

The notion that actually the whole story is going to stop—meaning: *oops, done, act three, over, closing shop*—**actually violates the very nature of the evolutionary impulse itself.**

So we're not involved in a kind of overly idealistic, impractical Don Quixote,[19] *let's take our horse and charge the windmill*—although there's some of that, admittedly. But it's much deeper, right? Everything we're doing is, in some fundamental way, *backed by the Universe.*

That's shocking. That's exciting. There's a plot line.

FROM PRE-TRAGIC TO TRAGIC: HOMO AMOR FEELS THE WHOLE

So I go from the pre-tragic to the tragic. I face the tragic. And to face the tragic means, for example, that I can't move out of Covid and forget that, for at least half a billion people, their lives got shattered, and then think that Covid's over.

---

19   Don Quixote is the hero of the novel *Don Quixote* by Miguel de Cervantes. He is an idealistic but misguided knight who often mistakes reality for fantasy. In a famous scene, he attacks windmills, believing they are giants. His name inspired the word "quixotic," meaning overly idealistic or impractical.

How did Pastor Martin Niemöller say it in the end of World War II?

First, they came for the communists, and I didn't speak out because I wasn't a communist.

Then they came for the socialists, and I didn't speak out because I wasn't a socialist.

And then they came for the trade unionists, and I didn't speak out because I wasn't a trade unionist.

And then they came for the Jews, and I didn't speak out because I wasn't a Jew.

Then they came for me, and there was no one left to speak out for me.

Homo amor means I can feel the whole.

There's a phrase in the beautiful language of Iran, from the beautiful people of Iran, a phrase called *Baraye*. *Baraye* means "For the sake of." In other words, it means *for the sake of the whole.*

That's the beginning of the movement from the tragic to the post-tragic. I begin to feel whole. My heart is broken, but somehow, I still have the capacity to celebrate.

And I don't wait until later to celebrate.

Langston Hughes, the Black poet, in the middle of the horror of the Black experience in some dimensions of the United States, writes, *What happens to a dream deferred? Does it dry up like a raisin in the sun?*

We can't wait to live the dream.

So we actually need to celebrate. We need to celebrate because *I can't change the world unless I'm willing to already live now in the world that's already changed. I can't liberate the world unless I'm willing to be Homo amor now.*

CHAPTER FOUR

HOMO AMOR INJUNCTION TWO: LAUGH OUT OF ONE SIDE OF YOUR MOUTH AND CRY OUT OF THE OTHER SIDE

LIVING THE DREAM

Our second injunction is: *Homo amor* laughs out of one side of her mouth and cries out of the other side of her mouth.

Homo amor, no matter where he/she is, does what the Hebrew lineage calls *Sabbath,* every seven days. *Homo amor* can practice in any language or in any lineage. But *Sabbath* means: *I live the dream.*

Homo amor lives the dream.

Langston Hughes, the black poet, writes:

> *What happens to a dream deferred?*
> *Does it dry up*
> *like a raisin in the sun?*
> *Or fester like a sore—*
> *and then run?*
> *Does it stink like rotten meat?*
> *Or crust and sugar over—*

like a syrupy sweet?

Maybe it just sags like a heavy load.

Or does it explode?

That's what happens when you stay in the tragic.

You can't stay in the tragic.

You can't—like so many of my friends have done—become a *doomer*.

You can't lose the vitality, joy, and hope that understands, *there's an evolutionary impulse.*

And evolution means the possibility of possibility, that's what evolution means. Evolution is the divine force of value, which is the possibility of possibility.

So **we have to live the dream now. And it's only from that place of living the dream, crying out of one side of my mouth and laughing out of the other, that it begins to become alive.**

What happens to a dream deferred?

The answer is, you can't defer the dream, you've got to *live* the dream.

***Homo amor* lives the dream now.**

1. *Homo amor* lets her heart be broken, moving from the pre-tragic to the tragic.
2. *Homo amor* is filled with hope, not because I'm a starry-eyed unrealist, but because *Homo amor* is backed by the Universe, which is the fourth Big Bang. That's what *Homo amor* is. Can you feel that? ***Homo amor* is the inherent structure of Reality unfolding in the fourth Big Bang.**

The truth is that the only thing that never changes is that it always changes. But to do that, I have to first take in the pain. I have to be able to hold the pain every day for ten minutes, and to enter into it so deeply in those ten minutes that my heart breaks.

And then, I have to *cast out remorse* and celebrate.

William Butler Yeats' poem:

> *When such as I cast out remorse,*
> *so great a sweetness fills my breast.*
> *We can dance and we can sing.*
> *We are blest by everything.*
> *And everything we look upon is blest.*

That's the place we move from. That's the beginning of the movement from the tragic to the post-tragic.

We conclude this step with the Iranian song *Baraye*.

Tomaaj Salehi, the beautiful rapper in Iran, was sentenced to death. Absurdly, insanely. His dear friend, Shervin Hajipour, writes *Baraye*. Shervin was arrested, released, and arrested again. *Baraye* is written after Mahsa Amini was brutally killed by the forces of repression.

What does it mean to be *Homo amor*, to feel *Baraye, for the sake of the whole?*

Baraye. For the sake of the whole.

Breathe it in.

Feel *Homo amor* being born.

In you. In me. It's not born in someone else.

It's that little moment where I let go. I'm in the fullness of my power, but I'm also surrendered to my own beauty, to my own depth.

Then *Homo amor* begins to be born.

MOVING FROM THE TRAGIC TO THE POST-TRAGIC

I got a long letter from one of my closest, dearest friends over the last decade. We met when he was in a more agnostic phase, and we got together to have a series of private conversations to prepare for a public discussion. Then that private conversation went deeper. He enrolled me in a number of key visions; I enrolled him in some vision of *Homo amor*. And he shifted from an agnostic position to a very different position.

And somewhere around 2015—it wasn't as formal as I'm about to describe— but we kind of said, "Let's part ways publicly. You go work on exteriors, and I'll go work on interiors." And he's been deep in this conversation. He just wrote me a very long letter—a stream of consciousness, you know, with ten flowcharts attached, as he tends to do—basically saying, "I don't think there's a way." I actually just read the whole thing through. And he said, "Of course, I'm going to continue," but he went through an enormous amount of information, and he said, "I don't actually rationally see a way."

He's one of the best thinkers in the world today. One of my dearest friends. I'm tempted to share a part of the letter with you—I won't, mostly because it's a private letter—but I also don't quite know how to communicate just how serious it is.

So **we're going to move to the post-tragic.** This next section is our last conversation for now on the tragic before we shift modes. But I will just say one thing.

Based on every rational faculty that I have—having read a thousand books, literally, without exaggeration, and having read five thousand papers, and having talked to the best people in the world, looked at this year after year—I **don't rationally believe that there's a way through without an emergence that spreads through the world of the kind that we're describing here.**

In other words, **if *Homo sapiens* remains *Homo sapiens*, we will not get through.** There's no question about it. It's just not going to happen.

And at the same time, **the hope, the possibility of becoming *Homo amor* is so gorgeous and so real.**

So all of us here together, as we are thinking, feeling, and practicing together in the *dharma*.[20]

I want to say just one more thing before move on. I don't want to go down this road, but it just needs to be said.

There's one very big deal that just needs to be on the table, which is:

The death of humanity is not a bigger challenge to my experience of the goodness of the world than the death of a human being.

In other words, the death of *any* innocent human being—and particularly the *brutal* death of any innocent human being, any place in the world—the first shock of existence—**the brutal death of any innocent human being is as much of a challenge to the goodness of Reality as the death of humanity itself.**

That's a shocking sentence because the nature of value is that it's not measured, it's not quantified. We're so conditioned to quantify. We're so conditioned to commodify. We're so conditioned to measure.

◆ But the way we hold the death of an individual human being—and its an unbearable tragedy, when that death is unjust or cruel, violent, or torturous—it's not with some form

---

20   We are not using the word *dharma* in the sense of the Hinduist, Buddhist, or Kashmir Shaivite expression, a Sanskrit word meaning something like universal law. Rather, we are using it in the sense of a post-postmodern comprehensive teaching, the new Story that is an integration of the best of the premodern, modern, and postmodern realizations, a new set of First Principles and First Values of Cosmos that are woven together to a new Universe Story with its corollary narratives of identity, community, power, sexuality, etc.

of theology that explains why it's okay; instead, we hold it with a shattered heart.

- We also hold the unbearable goodness and joy of Reality for lots of very potent, powerful, and compelling reasons—because it lives deep in our first-person.

We hold both of those together. One doesn't nullify the other. **We laugh out of one side of our mouth, we cry out of the other.**

That's the nature of this moment—being able to hold those two and not turn away. Can you feel that?

To not turn away from either side.

TO DEAL WITH EXISTENTIAL RISK, THE SUBJECT HAS TO BECOME OBJECT

We're going to do one more conversation on existential risk to really understand it. We're going to move from first-person to third-person. **It's only when a subject becomes object that I can operate on it.** So if a subject is inside of me, and I can't see it, it's not object. I can't operate on it. Does that make sense?

So here's an easy example of how subject has to become object to be able work with it.

The first person I ever did a piece of inner work with, when I was like 21 or 22 years old, owns the big lighting fixture family company in California, and he's a great guy. But when it came to negotiating with his employees for raises or compensation, he got very hard and very brittle.

After a relatively short period of time, we realized that his dad, who he loved dearly, his dad's voice was in him. And his dad always told him, "Don't be soft, be a real man when you have to deal with the staff." So he was this totally sweet, lovely guy. But then, when it came time for the negotiation—

although he didn't actually hear his dad's voice—he was making sure his dad loved him.

So that was *subject* that had to become *object*. It had to be on the table and then we could work with it. Does that make sense?

So it is the same thing with existential risk. If subject—this thing— doesn't become object, if we can't see it in front of us, then we can't work with it.

So in the first chapter, we worked with it in first-person, which no one ever does. We actually *felt* it. We faced in. Now let's step out. Let's look *at* it.

Does that make sense? Can you feel the difference in the move?

I'm going to make a few short steps. And again, we're going to cover an enormous amount of ground. Every single word and sentence matters. Because I want to get the precise pieces that we need to become *Homo amor.* That's all we want to do.

NOT A POLY-CRISIS BUT A META-CRISIS

A lot of people talk about existential risk as a *poly-crisis.* Poly-crisis means there are multiple vectors—lots of things are happening. There's a cascading risk landscape. There are risks happening in multiple dimensions that all impact each other. It's a poly-crisis that's exploding.

I think it's a mistake. **It's not a poly-crisis—although that's accurate—it's a meta-crisis.**

You might say, *What the fuck is the difference? Why do I really care whether they call it a poly-crisis or a meta-crisis?* The answer is—it's everything. It's the whole difference.

Because if it's a poly-crisis, it's multiple issues. There are multiple factors, and you can't handle them. There's just too much going on. It's all contradictory. **If you get that it's a meta-crisis—meaning that there's a**

meta set of principles—you understand that there's something driving the whole thing.

Who remembers the show *House*? Remember, Doctor House? What was his deal? He was a little cranky, a little cantankerous. Actually, a loving guy, although somewhat obnoxious. But he was a beautiful guy. And what was his greatness? Diagnosis. He would diagnose—and that was always the breakthrough.

If you could actually see underneath the poly-crisis, you could see what's actually happening.

So we're going to be Dr. House here. We've got to do some diagnosis together. Otherwise, the whole conversation just doesn't take off.

So it's a meta-crisis—and that's hopeful. **You can't move from the tragic to the post-tragic if it's a poly-crisis.** We're just fucked. And then do what you do? But if it's a meta-crisis, it's hopeful.

THE GENERATOR FUNCTION FOR EXISTENTIAL RISK: RIVALROUS CONFLICT GOVERNED BY WIN-LOSE METRICS

So what's underneath?

What are the *generator functions* for existential risk?

"Generator function" is a term from engineering, meaning: *what causes it?*

What drives existential risk? There's a very simple equation, which is:

> *rivalrous conflict + exponential technology – a Field of Value*
> *= extinction*

That's the basic, very simple equation.

In other words, we've got eight billion people in the world today. What drives the action? What makes it move?

What drives the action in the world today is the success story. It's a collective story. It's a personal story. It's an individual story. It's a national story. It's a multinational corporation story. It's a small business story. It's a big business story.

But when all is said and done, what drives the overwhelming majority of human beings in the world today is rivalrous conflict. It's somehow *me against you, you against me*—whether it's in a family, on a team, or in a company. Whether I'm running a retreat center, or a company, or a grocery store, or I'm running a consulting firm—**what drives virtually the entire world, from China to Russia, to Europe, to family companies, to families, to individuals, is always rivalrous conflict.**

That is the driving force. That is the narrative that drives Reality. That's the narrative that Harari understands, and he's correct. That's rivalrous conflict.

Now, that's not new. But it's new in one sense. Today, there are lots of individuals playing the rivalrous conflict game—and it's not just religions.

There were always religions playing the rivalrous conflict game. But now it's religions, countries, blocs of countries, companies against companies, divisions against divisions in companies, and people on a team within a division in a company competing against each other.

It's a constant process of rivalrous conflict.

WE'RE A SECOND AWAY FROM PULLING A BLACK BALL FROM THE TECHNOLOGY URN

Now, if you're doing that with bows and arrows, you can only do X amount of damage.

I looked at a chart last week about the move from a musket to a rifle to a grenade to the first kind of bomb, to the available weaponry in the world today, which is being stockpiled all over the world.

The curve is that **we're moving towards exponential technology, in which we're exponentially increasing our capacities for destruction** and stockpiling them all over the world without safeguards of any real kind. **And this is available to rogue non-state actors on a constant basis**—from bioweapons to weaponized drones—and the list goes on and on.

Rivalrous conflict by itself can be very destructive. Genghis Khan killed 50 million people—11% of the world's population. It's unimaginable. And that was all on horseback.

- Every civilization fell. We didn't solve the rivalrous conflict issues.
- But now we have a global civilization driven by rivalrous conflict times exponential technology—**exponential technology of a kind that's not regulated by state actors.**

Do you get that last sentence?

And if you want to make a nuclear bomb, that's kind of hard. You need uranium, you need to transport it, and you need a kind of state power. Look, Iran's not having such an easy time. There's been a big race. *Can Iran actually create a nuclear weapon, or can't they?* That tells you that it takes something. And there's an entire international game that can be played around a nuclear weapon.

Nick Bostrom asked a simple question. He wrote an essay in 2019 called *The Vulnerability Hypothesis.* This is the best way I can summarize it for you in a second.

He said essentially, developing a technology is like reaching into an urn and pulling out a ball at random. You have an urn, you put your hand on the urn, you get out a technology:

- Sometimes the technology is a white ball. You solve smallpox. It's pretty good.
- Sometimes you get a gray ball. Internal combustion engine,

cars—fantastic. Aside from the fact that all the wars of the 20th century employed the internal combustion engine, which exponentially increased maiming, damage, and devastation. So it's a gray ball. It's much more complex. Social media was certainly a gray ball in a thousand different ways.

- What if you get a black ball? Black ball means a technology that's very quickly deployable—it takes maybe a month or two to put together—and it's available to rogue non-state actors, and it has the power of nuclear destruction.

That's called a black ball.

We're a second away from that.

Literally a second away, not a minute away. We're a second away from it. Just to give you a sense.

And there's no governing Field of Value that actually operates in the hearts and minds of human beings that says, *No, don't do that.* **It doesn't exist.**

The assumption is, writes Yuval, that *if humans disappear, it doesn't matter.* And *all values are made up,* and *human rights are made up.* I just want you to get the effect of that. *Human rights are contrived, made up. They're not real. Nothing's real. Love's not real. It's all contrivance.*

So then you play the power game. Why not?

Remember what we said? We said:

- You've got the doomer position.
- You've got the denial position.
- What's the third position? Domination.

Domination is rivalrous conflict. That's the domination move. And that move is being played all over the place.

How many people here have cell phones? So here's a piece of news—a couple of million people have died for your cell phones. Go to Congo and see what's happening in today in order to get the necessary raw materials—cobalt, etc.—for our cell phones. We don't place our attention on it. We just keep using our cell phones and all our apps.

All the information is available. We ignore it. **Our cell phones have caused massacres, torture, the equivalent of concentration camps, mass rapes.** All that information is objectively available, but we're not even aware of it. But that's actually what cell phones cause. We basically turn away and participate in this rivalrous conflict. And all of us, one way or the other, we may spend some time in personal development—but basically, we want to be *successful.*

Rivalrous conflict times exponential technology.

AI EXPONENTIATES THE GOALS OF RIVALROUS CONFLICT

Now, what's artificial intelligence? Do you want to know what AI is? **AI means that the technology continues to exponentiate towards the goals of rivalrous conflict—*by itself.* A nuclear weapon can't build a better nuclear weapon. It can't be done. AI builds a better nuclear weapon. And it's the entire system that's optimized towards rivalrous conflict—and then super-optimized, super-exponentially charged by AI, increasing the whole game at unimaginable rates of speed. That's what AI is.

The issue is not, *will AI rise up and become sentient and take over the world?* Don't worry about it. You don't have to lose a lot of sleep over that for quite a long time. That's not the issue. **The issue is that AI exponentiates already exponential vectors of destruction—with no one checking it out and no one standing against it.**

And we're literally breaths away from a world in which we're living inside a *planetary stack* (Benjamin Bratton's word), driven by AI, with no one to talk to, no recourse.

So that's existential risk, just to give you a sense.

Existential risk is rivalrous conflict times exponential technology equals extinction.

There's no way to break that formula unless you introduce something new in the formula. And what would you introduce that's new? **You'd have to introduce something new in the formula that changes one of the values in the formula in a fundamental way.** Is the core of that clear? In a certain sense, we're just beginning to cut through.

THE THREE RESPONSES TO EXISTENTIAL RISK: INFRASTRUCTURE, SOCIAL STRUCTURE AND SUPERSTRUCTURE

Now, let's close that door and open a completely different door. It's going to get us right to the middle.

So how do we respond? So there are three ways to respond here. There are three basic moves we can make.

One of them is **infrastructure.** Infrastructure would mean, for example, that we develop technologies that allow us to identify bioweapons in the wastewater. Okay, we can catch some bioweapons in the wastewater. That's good infrastructure. But it's not going to ultimately work. There will ultimately be technology that will outsmart that. You just need very narrow sectors of people to outsmart it. But it's a good idea. So we're all for infrastructure. Infrastructure is a great idea. You could try and approach existential risk through infrastructure.

Now, I just want to share with you—there's almost no one working on existential risk. I just want to start there. You would think there are these huge intergovernmental world offices sitting, paying attention to this. There's not. That's what's kind of shocking.

There are a few centers for existential risk—poorly funded, in the way-stations of a couple of universities.

Because everyone's engaged in rivalrous conflict:

- ◆ I'm a politician, I want to get reelected.
- ◆ I'm a multinational corporation, I'm looking at my short-term profit.

Actually, you would think this is being addressed. You would think that there's a global deep Manhattan Project in America to deal with existential risk. It doesn't exist.

I can't even begin to tell you what that means.

Do you remember Covid? Do you remember the big international conference where everyone got together to handle Covid? Well, you don't, because *it never happened.* It never happened.

Literally, you've got this virus that doesn't respect national boundaries, that is devastating the world. There's no vaccine. You would think that we'd get everyone together and sit around a table. You couldn't fucking get everyone to sit around a table because rivalrous conflict was too intense.

Someone called me in 2022 and said, "I'll give you a million dollars next week"—this is a true story—"if you can bring together, in a behind-doors conversation, the leading figures in science critiquing the vaccine process and leading people supporting the vaccine process."

We made contact over a week. No one would come to the table *behind* the scenes. Do you understand what that means? **We couldn't convene a conversation between the two sides.** We offered 10 people each $50,000 to fly in for two days. There would be no recording. There was no conference around Covid to figure out what to do; we couldn't get it together.

Covid was a little minor dress rehearsal. But it's just the beginning of the beginning. So there's **infrastructure.** You can and must do infrastructure work, but it's limited.

You can try to do **social structure** work, meaning changing law and regulating, but it's very hard to do social structure that overcomes rivalrous conflict.

I'll give you one example: There's this whole conversation going on in the world, saying *we're going to use AI to solve the world's problems.* In other words, we're going to create a superintelligence that's not invested with any sense of value to solve the world's problems. That's such a disaster. But let's bracket that problem.

But they say—the engineers, the data scientists, the machine intelligence experts—that *they* are going to work to solve all these great issues. There are about 10,000 data scientists in the world who are worth their salt. None of them have jobs at universities. Virtually not one. Where do they work?

They don't work at public hospitals.

They don't work at universities.

The best minds in the world are all working for the tech sector.

The tech sector has completely bought the 10,000 minds that could actually work on a set of these issues.

The government can't regulate AI because there's no one in the entire government who has even a vague sense of how large language models work. You can't regulate something you don't understand. **And the reason no one understands it is because the very few people who do understand it are all making money on it.** Not even a lot of money, a million bucks a year—big fucking deal, right?

But no, the notion that *I would give that up for a larger Field of Value* is absurd to virtually all 10,000 people. Does everyone get that?

We have a complete brain drain and heart drain, where everyone is drawn into the win-lose metrics. So social structure is important. Meaning, changing laws is important. And regulation is important. For example, thalidomide was this miracle cure for morning sickness, but it turned out that good research wasn't done, and it deformed babies in the early 60s. The reason it didn't enter the United States was that one regulator actually stood against it. **So regulation is important.** But we don't have regulators who have any idea now what's going on. We don't have regulation in any effective way.

So social structure and infrastructure are important but limited.

But there's a third possibility—and I'm borrowing these terms from Marvin Harris.[21] The third possibility is *superstructure.* Superstructure is a fancy word. It means a lot of things. But I'm going to translate it into what I think its essence should be: Superstructure means *we all live in a story. We all live inside a story. We all live inside a Story of Value.*

When I change the superstructure,[22] when I evolve the Story of Value, then everyone begins to generate Reality together from within this new story.

I would say the primary thing that Yuval Harari and I agree on is this fact. For Yuval, however, the stories are made up. So Yuval says, *just manipulate the people,* essentially. *Switch the story, and you'll get a better result.* But of course, that doesn't work. In a world that's completely interconnected, propaganda doesn't work anymore. **You can't foist a story on people.**

WE RECOGNIZE IN OUR INTERIORS THAT STORIES ARE REAL, VALUE IS REAL

What I'm saying is—based on an enormous amount of information—that:

---

21 Marvin Harris, *Cultural Materialism: The Struggle for a Science of Culture* (Walnut Creek: AltaMira Press, 2001—first published 1979).

22 For a deeper understanding of infrastructure, superstructure, and social structure, see David J. Temple, *First Principles and First Values* (2024).

- Stories are *real*.
- There are Stories of Value.
- There are stories that are aligned with the nature of the Cosmos.
- There's an evolution of Reality in which there is a new emergent story.
- This is actually a story that lives in people, that they recognize, and that they can participate in.

Not because *I said so*. Who cares what I say?

- Because it's true.
- Because we participate in it.
- Because we recognize it.
- Because we yearn for it.
- Because we long for it.

And we all know in our interior knowing that that's true. In moments of deep practice and moments of deep heart-opening, we can feel it. On *the inside of the inside* we are actually not driven by rivalrous conflict or exponential technologies.

We are driven by something else.

So the one vector that can actually shift everything is the emergence of a new story. But a new story is not a made-up story.

It's not a postmodern *we made up a new story*.

It's actually a new story that integrates the best scientific information, interior science and exterior science, across all ages and all disciplines, **integrated into a second simplicity beyond complexity** that we can tell, feel, share, and be—all over China, all over the United States, all over Russia, all over Gaza, all over Tel Aviv, all over Montana, all over Europe, and all over the entire world.

A NEW STORY OF VALUE CHANGES EVERYTHING

But we *can* shift the whole thing.

How? The only way that things ever shifted.

We live and become a new story.

That's what happened in the Renaissance. That's actually what happened at that time between worlds and time between stories. The nine families sitting around Florence said, *It can't change.* This one group of people said, *No, we're going to actually resource in some serious way.* Not as a little side project. The Medici's took it on as their major project. They said, *We care about this as much as we care about profit.*

They actually stepped out of the Medici rivalrous conflict, and they said, *the Medici family is committed to creating a memory of the future.*

And they did. And they created the Florentine Platonic Academy with Ficino and da Vinci.

And instead of *doomer*, instead of *domination*, and instead of *denial*, there was *a new dawn.*

And that dawn was called **modernity**. And all of the best of universal human rights, the best of the feminine, the best of embodiment, the best of everything that we experience in large measure comes out of that new story told.

But that new story was before there was exponential technology, when there was still a memory that *value was real.*

Now the assumption is that value is just not real. So what do we do?

Now we're going to take one huge, hard, easy, gentle, sweet, complex, even more simple leap. And if we don't take this leap, the whole thing doesn't work, and we're just building castles in the sand.

It's actually very simple. But if we can make this leap, then the whole thing will work.

We do this by introducing the notion of **a new Story of Value.**

Value begins to arouse my will.

It begins to arouse my political will, my moral will, and my economic will.

And it actually overrides, bypasses, and even inhibits rivalrous conflict governed by win-lose metrics.

That's a big deal.

I'm going to give you a really crazy dumb example and a tragic one.

In Europe, there's a particular line where French and German soldiers fired at each other throughout World War I and about 5 million people were killed. And they were sitting there, firing at each other, you know, 100 yards away.

Why did they stay? *Hello? Could we, like, desert?* There are no computers that are going to track you. You slip into the forest—French forest, Belgian forest—and you just have to find your way out of there. But almost no one deserted. Isn't that insane? You're literally sitting there. You see people being killed all around you. And you stay.

And I did a deep-dive research with my son at one point on the rates of desertion—they are virtually non-existent.

Why did they stay? **They stayed because they had a sense of value**—that was indeed completely distorted, completely corrupted, and completely fucked up.

That's true. They all should have stopped, for sure. But that's not my point.

My point is that *even a distorted sense of value has enormous power.*

RECLAIMING VALUE: A HERO STANDS FOR VALUE

The reason we rebelled against value was because its distorted forms did so much damage. Does everyone get that sentence?

Because its distorted forms did so much damage, we said, "Fuck value." That was one of the about three reasons—we'll get to the more important one in a moment.

So we threw value out, and we said, *we'll just live lives of rational self-interest.* But actually, that doesn't work—because rational self-interest becomes rivalrous conflict governed by win-lose metrics. So I just want to use that simple example to point out that **value is powerful.** It's very powerful.

What would we do for our loved ones, people we love madly, and closely, and dearly? We'd stand for them. We might even risk our lives for them. Why? **Because there's value inside of us that actually overrides this notion of win-lose conflict.**

What is a hero? **A hero is someone who stands for value.** That's why we like heroes.

A hero is valiant. A hero has valor.

- What's the root word of valor and valiant? Value.
- What's the other root word? Be my Valentine. *Valentius.* Love. Eros. So the hero embodies this sense of *Value, Love,* and *Eros.*
- And therefore, the hero's life is *valid.*
- The hero has a unique *valence,* which is a unique sense of combining the *valence* of electrons, the *valence* of Eros.
- Because the hero is filled with *value,* which fills him with *valor* and *valiance.*

It's a beautiful word—hero. That's why Marvel hero movies are huge in the world in the middle of postmodernity.

Why do we love heroes? Because heroes know something. What do they know? **They know there's this larger Field of Value, and we can stand for it.**

Heroes are early adopters of Homo amor. The democratization of the hero is Homo amor.

So what happened? **Why did we all throw value out in postmodernism?** For a very simple reason.

Okay, now stay close for a second. And we've got to solve it, or the whole thing falls. Everything we're doing—everything—just collapses.

VALUE IS BOTH ETERNAL AND IT EVOLVES

Someone sent me a book a while ago called *The Global Revolt,* written by a lovely young man, a friend of my daughter's in Israel who is an international reporter. Just a beautiful, intelligent, classical expression of the modern world. And he writes in the book something like, *of course, none of us can hold the truth of value anymore.*

He says, "Of course"—that's a given. *Because we all know that there's no such thing as a universal, preordained, and eternal value.* Preordained, meaning *this is it,* it never changes; eternal, unchanging. He says, *We all know that's ridiculous.* Now, he's right, actually. In other words, the claim of the premodern religions was that there's preordained and eternal value, and *I happen to own it and they don't.*

So whether we're talking about sexuality, whether we're talking about commerce, whether we're talking about any part of ethics, or whether we're talking about how you should live, pray, and breathe, here's what **premodernity** says about value:

- ✦ It's preordained.
- ✦ It's always been this way from the beginning of time.
- ✦ It's unchanging.
- ✦ It's eternal.
- ✦ It never changes.

Along comes **modernity** and says, *No, there is evolution.* Things change. Things move. Things shift. And evolution destroys eternal value. There can't be an eternal Tao, because how could there be an eternal Tao if everything's evolving? That's the fastest way I could say a thousand pages.

In other words, if I were to say that value means something imprinted in Reality from the beginning, something that cannot change—then it's not just that love is a value, but that love never changes; it's eternal; its nature is fixed and unchanging.

Let's say I believe in a particular form of Christian love, and that form excludes people who are not Christian in a specific way. They're excluded from the story—because we are the chosen people, and they are not. That is what value means in that framework.

Or take the idea that only one kind of sexuality is permitted, and all others are forbidden—because value is seen as absolute and unchanging.

But then we realize, *No, that's not true.* Actually, there's this emergence, there's this shifting. Things are actually shifting, and changing, and emerging in a beautiful way. So then we said, *There can't be an eternal Tao.*

By the Tao, what I mean is—although not all Taoists would agree—but the way I'm reading the Tao is: **the Tao is the Field of Value. It's the ground of being.** It's that which underlies everything—the Tao, from ancient Taoism. So I'm using the Tao as a general term for the **Field of Value.**

So we talk about the *eternal* Tao. It's eternal. But here's the big move:

The eternal Tao is the evolving Tao.

Simple. I thought about it day and night for a decade. I called my friend Ken, and we were ecstatic about it. We just did 12 dialogues about it, and we just published a book on this called *First Principles and First Values*, which changes the entire game.

What does it mean? It means love is eternal; love is a real value of the Cosmos. That's why all the songs are love songs—because the music of Reality is a love song.

Love is real. And love means something.

- It means I care for you.
- It means I hold you.
- It means I nurture you.
- It means I try and take care of you.
- It means I'm sensitive to you.

But *how* that value of love plays out—*that evolves*. There is an evolution of love. In other words, one of the values of Cosmos is: it doesn't happen all in a lifetime. It happens over several lifetimes. It happens over history.

So one: value is Eros. Reality is Eros. Reality is this force of Eros, of love, of embrace, which is this movement that governs all of Reality—all the way up and all the way down, from subatomic particles to you and me. It's everywhere. Reality is Eros. Reality is love. But it's *Evolutionary* Love. It's the heart of existence itself.

And two: value *evolves*, so:

- Value is real. Reality is coded with value, which we all kind of know is true.
- And yet, value evolves.[23]

Love is real. Love evolves.

---

23 For a deeper read of "eternal and evolving value," see David J. Temple, *First Principles and First Values* (2024) and *Eternal and Evolving Value* (forthcoming 2026)

I participate in the evolution of love.

There's a Field of Eros. There's a Field of Eros Value.

I live in that field. That field lives in me.

And it evolves through me. It evolves through me.

What that means is that the whole game changes.

Because all of a sudden, **value is real—and value becomes the ground of a new universal shared Story of Value.** A shared Story of Value can inhibit rivalrous conflict because there is something deeper.

Last sentence, last example. Imagine I'm madly in love with my romantic beloved. That overrides everything else. I'll do everything for it. So then, imagine I had that same sense of mad love, but it was bigger and wider. I would be *Homo amor,* and I could actually feel the whole, and I felt not an ordinary romantic love—**I felt an Outrageous Love burning in me.**

And imagine I wasn't told that that was an *illusion*, and I wasn't told that it was *meaningless*.

But actually, we brought the best sciences to bear to realize that that's in fact the most meaningful truth.

And then that begins to become a shared Story of Value.

That's the beginning of the evolution of love.

That's the beginning of response to the meta-crisis.

BARAYE—FOR THE SAKE OF THE WHOLE

Homo amor, for the sake of the whole. We've looked at the song *Baraye,* for the sake of the whole. I can open my heart so wide, I can feel the whole thing.

Baraye, **for the sake of the whole.**

Baraye, a protest song after Mahsa Amini's death.

We're in Florence. We're in a time between worlds, we're in a time between stories.

There were only a thousand people involved in the Renaissance. And we're becoming the new story.

Remember when George Floyd was killed in the United States. People poured into the streets because they sensed that **value has been violated.**

Mahsa Amini was killed in Iran. People pour into the streets because there is a sense that a value had been violated and needs to be honored and defended.

There are three powerful versions of Baraye, we encourage you to listen to:

Baraye (original version by Shervin Hajipour)

For Woman, Life, Liberty (Baraye)—English version by Rana Mansour

Baraye (video clip with beautiful images of protests)

THE LYRICS TO BARAYE IN ENGLISH:

For dancing in the alleys and the streets
For the thrill and the fear of getting caught kissing
For my sister, my brother in unity
For all the times we tried to change their minds and stale beliefs
For the loss of pride, for poverty

For the dream of just a normal life for you and me
For all the children who are starving for a loaf of bread
For the greed of politics and all the lies they spread
For all the mass polluted air we breathe
For all the litter in the streets and all the dying trees
For all the animals who suffer from elimination
For all the cats and dogs who love us without no conditions
For all the tears that seem to never end
For all the images that keep on turning in our heads
For a simple smile to last a little while
For the future generations fighting for their time
For empty promises of heaven in the afterlife
For all the imprisonment of beautiful minds
For all the babies who were born and for the ones who died
For all the times you told the truth and all the times you lied
For all the speeches that we heard about a million times
For all the shacks and shelters that were sold to make a dime
For just a glimpse of a peaceful life
For the rising of the sun after an endless night
For all the pills we pop just to get some sleep
For all mankind and our country
For all the boys and girls who never knew equality
For woman, for life, liberty.
For liberty. For liberty. For liberty.

It's not rivalrous conflict; it is for the whole thing.

And she knows it.

And he knows it.

And the face of every girl and boy and man and woman in the protest, they knew it.

It is backed by the Universe. We're not making it up. It's already true. It's not an imposed story; it's not an arbitrary story. It's a story that we already know is true, but we haven't articulated. And then the story gets dismissed because *value is not real*, as value is only seen as *eternal* value—which it can't be.

No, the eternal value is the evolving value.

The eternal Tao is the evolving Tao.

CHAPTER FIVE

HOMO AMOR'S RESPONSE TO WHERE, WHO, AND WHAT?

THERE ARE SIMPLE FIRST PRINCIPLES IN THE EXTERIORS AND IN THE INTERIORS

We're now stepping into *Homo amor*. Who is *Homo amor*?

The three great questions of CosmoErotic Humanism are: *Where are we?*, *Who are we?*, and *What ought be done*? *Homo amor* is the response to *Who are we?* But first I want to tell you why we're looking at these questions.

I want to start with a meditation, which is an image of birds. This image of birds is going to guide pretty much everything we want to say and everything we want to do.

So, what do we see here? A murmuration.

How do the birds know what to do? How do you create the beauty of coherent complexity, which is coordinated, which discloses unimaginable grace and beauty? The birds don't have a GPS. There's no AI program collating and integrating information.

The birds are essentially following simple First Principles and First Values.

And they are:

1. Stay close to your nearest neighbor.
2. Don't fly too close.
3. Fly towards the center.

Wow. That's it.

Now, I want to catch this—this is a big deal.

There is a movie called *The Imitation Game*, which is about the code cracker, Turing, an English mathematician, who cracks the Nazi codes during World War II using his mathematical model of computation. His simple mathematical computational device was called *the Turing machine.*

It's a tragic, beautiful story. Turing is one of my great heroes. He had this panoramic, gorgeous mind. He was a gorgeous human being.

Turing went to Bell Labs (a research and development company) just a few years before he died in 1952, and he wrote an essay called *The Chemical Basis of Morphogenesis.* It is almost intractable. I'm going to try and simplify it in a couple of sentences.

What is Turing talking about?

- How do you create coherence, resonance out of vast complexity?
- How do we have any coordination in the world?
- How do we have any coherent complexity when we've got this vast array of separate parts?
- How can it possibly coordinate?

The mathematics of Turing's *Morphogenesis* is important, but if you cut through, he's basically saying something like: **there are simple first rules.**

And he's talking about exteriors and interiors. We call them First Principles and First Values, a new term we coined a few years ago, but it refers to the same thing. There are simple first rules. **And when you iterate them again**

and again, repeat them again and again, you then get coherence. Well, that is a big deal.

So, **coherence comes from the iteration of simple first rules** in exteriors. And as I was reading Turing about 15 years ago, I realized:

> *Just like there are simple first rules in exteriors, there are simple First Principles and First Values in interiors.*

Of course. Obviously.

There are lots of names for them—*Four Noble Truths* in Buddhism is probably one of them. The *Ten Commandments* was probably another take at it. But you get what everyone was going for?

Now, if we make a postmodern mistake and say that there's no Field of Value, then all those rules have to be made up. Then they can only be made up in a closed society, where some group of powerful people imposes them. However, closed societies become both stronger and weaker simultaneously as they violate an aspect of human nature. **In an open society, you face one of two possibilities: either it all falls apart, or open societies spiral out of control because there's nothing to cohere them.**

Alternatively, we can realize that underlying all societies is a set of simple first rules—simple First Principles and First Values—that have the capacity to cohere the whole thing.

THE EXILE OF VALUE TO COMMODIFIABLE VALUE

Do you remember the movie *Avatar 2*? Do you remember what were called *the Tulkans?* Tulkans are the name of a species of whale that went extinct through human predatory whale hunting.

The Tulkans were those huge whales in the movie. And they went to kill them because they had Amrita. And if you were wealthy enough, you could take some Amrita and have some form of eternal life. So that's basically about whales and whale oil, right? Obviously.

So why would someone kill a whale for whale oil? Because there's no Field of Value. Then, when you look at the whale, the only value that you see is the commodifiable value—the measurable value—of whale oil. So we almost killed all the whales in the world because we couldn't see this amazingly, shockingly beautiful, intense, gorgeous, wildly intelligent, feeling creature who is—literally—writing symphonies that are carried across the ocean.

We couldn't see any of it. We couldn't hear the symphonies. We couldn't hear the music. We couldn't feel the whale. Because we were in rivalrous conflict governed by win-lose metrics. And if I actually harpooned a whale, I got this little thing of whale oil that gave me one tiny notch in the rivalrous conflict. We exiled value to commodifiable value.

The entire system is oriented around simple first rules which are anti-value, anti-erotic, and anti-intimate. The entire system is oriented around rivalrous conflict governed by win-lose metrics.

What could be more anti-intimate and anti-erotic?

In rivalrous conflict, if we're friends, we might give each other a hug, but it's instrumental. It really is rivalrous conflict. In reality, it's about: *what advantage do I have?* This deadens and undermines the very structure of my own interior aliveness.

You may think that's nothing. You may think, "Oh, whatever, it's just a psychological issue. I'll go to a yoga retreat, I'll do some tantra, and I'll be okay."

No. That's *the entire system*. Do you get it?

Rivalrous conflict through win/lose metrics is the simple first rule that's iterated again and again and again, with exponential power through

exponential technology. And that governs the entire system because there's nothing else in the system to stand against it. And that leads to extinction.

THE FIRST GREAT QUESTION OF COSMOEROTIC HUMANISM: WHERE ARE WE?

The three great questions of CosmoErotic Humanism are:

- ◆ Who am I? Who are we?
- ◆ Where am I? Where are we?
- ◆ What's mine to do? What's ours to do? What ought to be done?

Now, we'll address the first question: *Where are we?*

So we said, in order to inhibit our existential risk equation, we need to actually add a dimension or rewrite the equation.

Rivalrous conflict + Exponential technology – Field of Value = Extinction.

What are the simplest first rules and first principles? They are the responses to three of the most elemental questions in the world that we all ask: *Where? Who? What?*

And notice, I'm not asking *why are we here.* I don't fucking care. *Why* is a theological question. Everyone's making it up. Forget about *why.* Put it aside. **The *why* will naturally emerge out of the *where* and the *who* and the *what.***

So let's look now at *where?* Earlier, we looked at the *where* of the *immediate where.* Where are we *right now?* Let's broaden our *where.*

Where are we? Where am I? Where do I live?

I'm going to put it in two equations and give a couple of examples. This is the short version of it, so we'll get a sense of it.[24]

---

24 For a deeper understanding, see David J. Temple, *First Principles and First Values* (2024).

Reality is not merely a fact. Reality is a story.

And stories are not made up—**stories are the very structure of Reality.** Muriel Rukeyser, the beautiful poet who wrote, *The Universe is made of stories, not atoms*—that is not quite true—but **atoms are stories as well.** It's all stories. We'll explain that in a second.

Reality is not merely a fact. Reality is a story.

Reality is not an ordinary story. Reality is a love story.

And now we're integrating the best sciences that we have across all platforms—pre-modern, modern, and post-modern—across all disciplines.

Reality is Eros, all the way up and all the way down the evolutionary chain.

But Reality is not an ordinary love story; it is not a romantic love story between two people. That's beautiful, but that is an exile of love. That takes love out of the cosmic fabric. It exiles love into only the human realm. And then it says: *In the human realm, it's only a particular kind of love: infatuation*—and that you're only allowed to do that with one person in a particular way. And if doing that with one person doesn't fill your whole life the way it did in the beginning, somehow your life is a failure.

It's an exile of love—which is why it crashes. Of course, it does. How could it not crash?

We have exiled love:

- From the Cosmos into the human world.
- From the human world into a very particular dimension of the human world.
- And that particular dimension of the world, in a particular stage—infatuation.
- And then it's supposed to last that way forever, or you're basically fundamentally flawed. And your essence and your life were a failure.

Because *after we've devalued the whole world, we left you a booby prize of romantic love. And if that doesn't work, you've got nothing.*

No!

> Reality's not merely a fact. Reality's a story.
>
> Reality's not an ordinary story. Reality's a love story—not love as *mere human sentiment, a social construction that looks a particular way at a particular age.*
>
> Reality's not an ordinary love story. Reality's an Evolutionary Love Story. Reality's an Outrageous Love Story.
>
> Reality is Eros, all the way up and all the way down.

And then, here's where it gets wild and crazy:

> My love story, your love story, is a chapter and a verse in the Universe: A Love Story.

My love story is not alienated, it's not separate from. I participate in the Field of Eros. Now, let's take to the next step.

REALITY IS THE EXPERIENCE OF RADICAL ALIVENESS, DESIRING

So let's look at, what is Eros? So here it gets crazy beautiful. Here's the Eros equation:

> *Eros = the experience of radical aliveness moving towards/desiring ever-deeper contact and ever-greater wholeness.*

Now, that's a very precise formula. We wrote it up in a much fancier way in the book *First Principles and First Values.*[25] That's a formula that took us 15 years to clarify.

---

25   For more interior science equations of CosmoErotic Humanism, see David J. Temple, *First Principles and First Values* (2024).

Eros is the experience of radical aliveness. It's moving towards—not just moving towards, though, it's *desiring*—Eros desires ever-deeper contact and ever-greater wholeness.

So now, imagine that the simple First Principles that govern my life are:

1. Rivalrous conflict.
2. Get more and more status.
3. Hide your desire, because there's something fundamentally shameful about it.

So instead of the three simple first rules that govern murmuration—the birds in the sky—we have these other three: rivalrous conflict, hide your real self, and certainly keep your desire out of sight. Those are the simple first rules that govern society—quite literally.

But actually, Reality is a love story. Reality is Eros. **That's the best science we have.**

There's a word we use, which is called *allurement*. It's not quite the same as *attraction*. *Allurement* is a similar word, but it's got a little more magic to it. Can you feel the difference?

It's *allurement*.

Attraction is almost mechanical. Science took the word *allurement* and wanted to make it sound more mechanical, so it called it *attraction*. **However, the scientific description of *attraction* is not just a way of describing the mechanics of the Cosmos, but also the *music* of the Cosmos.**

The *music* of Cosmos is *allurement*. Reality is allurement, all the way up and all the way down.

Why are you reading this book? Allurement. All the rational reasons fall to the wayside. It is some form of allurement to each other, to a vision, to a possibility. So Reality equals this experience of radical aliveness, desiring.

Reality is desire, it's Eros, moving towards ever-deeper contact and ever-greater wholeness.

Eros is the desire for more intimacy.

EVOLUTION IS THE PROGRESSIVE DEEPENING OF INTIMACIES

We go to school—biology class—and we're told, *evolution is a mechanical process going from simplicity to complexity*. I must have talked to a hundred evolutionary theorists over the last ten years. Everyone agrees that's an *insane* description, but it's just the way we describe it. **We describe the world as *mechanics.***

But what is evolution? In the best reading of science, evolution is the *progressive deepening of intimacies.*

And here's the last sentence in this flow.

Intimacy is a Value of Cosmos. *Eros* is a Value of Cosmos.

And what does *intimacy* mean?

Intimacy equals shared identity in the context of otherness.

1. And then we have this *mutuality of recognition*—we recognize each other.
2. This *mutuality of pathos*—we feel each other.
3. This *mutuality of value*—we have this shared value.
4. And this *mutuality of purpose*—we have a shared purpose.

The Intimacy Equation of CosmoErotic Humanism:

Intimacy = Shared Identity x [Relative] Otherness x Mutuality (Recognition + Feeling + Value + Purpose)

So let's just make this real.

We mentioned this earlier just in passing. It's 380,000 years after the Big Bang. I'm a proton, and I'm a neutron. I'm minding my own business. And then I feel this incredibly powerful drive. And I don't know if any of you have ever experienced a sexual drive, or maybe you know someone who has. So if you can imagine that person having that experience. Now, exponentiate that experience. You can feel this unimaginably powerful allurement, and the proton and the neutron come together, and they create a new *shared identity* in the context of *otherness*.

The proton and the neutron don't disappear. And they have *mutuality of recognition*. The proton and the neutron recognize each other. And they have *mutuality of pathos*. They feel each other. And they have a *mutuality of value*. They actually have a *shared Field of Value,* which allows them to come together. And then they have *mutuality of purpose*. They become a fucking *atom*. And an atom does stuff that protons and neutrons can't do separately. **So there's an entirely new *purpose.***

That's intimacy.

Does that sound strikingly similar to some experiences that we've had? Of course, it does. Is it the same? Of course not. I've never dated a proton—just saying. I don't want to share my whole dating history, but I've never dated a proton. So of course it's not the same; there's an *evolution of intimacy*. Obviously. And of course, intimacy is not the same between a proton and a neutron as between human beings in the third Big Bang. Obviously.

But it's the *same field.* That's the point.

It's the same Eros.

WE LIVE IN A FIELD OF EROSVALUE

And here's the thing. You can't say the word *Eros* without the word *Value*. I woke up one morning, and I realized, *We can't use the word Eros anymore without using the word Value.* You can't. It's *ErosValue*. It's one word. It's intimacy. It's *ErosValue*. It's one thing. It's one word.

So, back to the first question of CosmoErotic Humanism: *Where are we?*

- ◆ We're in a Field of ErosValue.
- ◆ We're in the Universe, which is a love story.
- ◆ We're in the Amorous Cosmos.
- ◆ We're in the Intimate Universe.
- ◆ We're in the Tao.
- ◆ We're in the Field of Value.

It's not a pre-modern field of value. It's not owned, it's not colonized, it's not commodified, it's not hijacked.

But all of us live—quite literally—ontologically, meaning *for real,* in a *Field of ErosValue.*

We live in a Field of LoveIntelligence, and LoveBeauty, and LoveDesire, that is the animating Eros and energy of All-That-Is.

That's the field.

That's the beginning of a *new story.* And it's a Story of Value—of intrinsic value, yet *evolving* value.

We've got the beginning of a response to the question: *Where are we?* **We live in a Field of *LoveIntelligence,* and *LoveBeauty,* and *LoveDesire,* that is the animating Eros and energy of All-That-Is.**

Value is not hard to find.

Value is impossible to avoid.

CHAPTER SIX

HOMO AMOR INJUNCTION THREE: YOUR STORY MATTERS

THE KEY IS THE NEW STORY OF VALUE

So if you're reading this book and you're just having a good time and then I completely failed. This should be terrifying. And I mean that only half-jokingly. In other words, **it's both ecstatic and terrifying**, right? If you're just on the ecstatic side or just on the terrified side, it doesn't work. But if we actually get it, it actually is terrifying.

But it's paradoxical.

My native source lineage is called the lineage of Solomon. I spent too many years locked in the Oxford Library reading Aramaic texts about the lineage of Solomon, which is my kind of home turf.

So Solomon's father, David, has a beautiful phrase where he says, *I tremble and I dance.* There's actually a trembling.

And a trembling has Eros, right? There's an Eros in trembling and there's a dance. It's ecstatic, but it has to be *ecstatically urgent.*

And I'm saying this because we're trying to evoke *Homo amor.*

I'm looking—together with you, as spiritual friends—for this quality of *Homo amor.* It's a particular quality.

So let's look at the next injunction:

1. First, *I let my heart be broken*. Injunction one.
2. Second, *I laugh out of one side of my mouth and I cry out of the other side of my mouth*. Injunction two.
3. And the third injunction is: *your story matters*.

Do you remember that movie in 1999 called *The Matrix*? In *Matrix 2*, there's the Keymaster. So, what is the key? The key means that **a new Story of Value is a key**.

It's a key. It's not about, *is it a great book at a particular moment, or is it interesting to me in this very moment*. No, it's *a key*. **It literally unlocks Reality because it matches Reality.**

It's precisely aligned. And if you can unlock and open the door, then you open new possibilities. But if you've ever had a key that didn't exactly work—and it's a precise copy of the key, but it's just one tad slightly off, then the door doesn't open, right? And there's an enormous amount of fundamentalist dogma and New Age dogma that is actually interesting, but the door doesn't open.

If the door doesn't open, we cannot create what we need to create: a universal grammar of value, a new Story of Value, as a context for our diversity. **This context inhibits rivalrous conflict from being the simple first rule, and instead, it reorients us towards value itself.** Do those sentences now make sense? So, we're going to try and take three *keymaster* steps.

STORY IS A VALUE OF REALITY

Story is a structure of Reality. In CosmoErotic Humanism we have this beautiful practice of tracing your personal story and writing your *sacred autobiography*.[26]

---

26   Read more about this practice in Marc Gafni, *The New Story of Value in Response to Existential Risk*, oral essays from Eros Mystery School 2019.

What do we mean when we say:

> Reality is not merely a fact. Reality is a story.

> Reality is not an ordinary story. It's a love story.

> It's not an ordinary love story. It's an *Evolutionary* Love Story.

> Your story—yours, mine—is chapter and verse in *The Universe: A Love Story.*

It's the Amorous Cosmos. The Intimate Universe. The CosmoErotic Universe. They're all pointing to the same thing.

1. ***Story* itself is a *value* of Reality**. It's a very big sentence.
2. We said before that *Eros* is a value of Reality; intimacy is a value of Reality.

EVOLUTION IS A VALUE OF REALITY

Evolution itself is a value of Reality.

And it's not just *eternal* Tao. It's an *evolving* Tao.

What's another word for evolution? *Transformation.* Evolution equals a series of transformations.

That's all it is. That's what I mean by *second simplicity.* When you cut through it, on the other side of complexity, it's actually simple. What is evolution? A series of transformations.

3. So now, our third value that we've elucidated is: *evolution itself is a value.*

So it's not, *evolution versus religion.* That is bullshit. **Evolution is a value of Reality.** That just changes everything. That's our third value.

Those are all *First Principles and First Values of Reality*, in the Field of Value.

Okay, now catch this. This is wild.

Okay, I was talking to Howard Bloom. Some of you know him. He wrote like eight, nine books. He's this insane, raving genius, who I love dearly. He's 80 years old. He was Michael Jackson's publicist and found Peter Gabriel and did this wild music thing for 15 years while he was writing probably the most insane, creative books in physics and sociology and cosmology. And he calls himself a *stone-cold atheist*. But he's an atheist like I'm the Pope. In other words, he's an atheist rebelling against the old version of religion. And he's kind of like the guru today of NASA in the United States.[27]

So, I said to Howard, *Story is a structure of Reality.*

And Howard says, *That's ridiculous.*

And at the end of the year, Howard wrote—and he's really the best scientific mind I know—**"Story is the structure of Reality."**

There's no other way to read science. It's a *big deal.*

THE STORY OF REALITY HAS A PLOTLINE

So, here's what story means. What is a story? A story means that there's an inherently related succession of events. Meaning it's not blind. It is not preordained either, but it's also not blind and accidental. There's an inherent plot line to the story—although it is not a preordained ending, there's not a puppeteer Divinity—there is a plot line, meaning it has a *telos*, it's going somewhere.

Story means *it's going somewhere. It has a direction.*

Now, *it's going somewhere* doesn't mean it's going to a Christian heaven— that's the reason why science rebelled against *telos*. It's not going to the Jewish afterlife. It's not going to some sort of *jihadi explosion.*

---

27   For a full introduction to Howard Bloom, see: "The Holy Heresy of Scientist Howard Bloom: Extended Preface for *The Case of the Sexual Cosmos*: Introducing Howard Bloom," on Substack: https://worldphilosophyreligion.substack.com/p/preface-by-marc-gafni-for-case-of-sexual-cosmos.

That's not what we mean by *it's going somewhere*.

We mean it has *direction*.

It's what we said earlier—we didn't just randomly get from quarks to culture, mud to Mozart, bacteria to Bach, or dirt to Dostoevsky.

1. There's a *direction*, there's a *plot line*, which means there's an *inherent relationship* between the events—they're not just blind.
2. The plot line is *driven by desire*—that's Eros.

THE PLOTLINE OF THE STORY IS TOWARDS MORE VALUE

So, what is the plot line that is driven by desire reaching for?

What does desire want?

Desire wants value.

- It wants more wholeness.
- It wants more goodness.
- It wants more depth.
- It wants more love.
- It wants more aliveness.

But as Alfred North Whitehead wrote, *the Cosmos is hungry*. He was afraid to use the word *desire* in Cambridge, so he talked about *the appetition of the Cosmos.*

The Cosmos has appetite. The Cosmos desires.

What does the Cosmos desire? Value.

So, the plot line of the story is value.

3. That means that the First Principles and First Values of Cosmos— if they indeed exist, which they do—are the plot lines of the story.

Eros Value is the plot line of the story, desiring/seeking more and more aliveness, more and more contact, and more and more wholeness.

So, in the practice of writing our sacred autobiography, we then trace this story in our personal life—which is the story of desiring more and more contact and more and more wholeness. It is not an isolated, alienated story.

The story of my life is me as a unique expression of the plot line of Reality itself.

Does that make sense?

All of a sudden, my life is not alienated, my life actually is chapter and verse in the story of Cosmos.

- One of the plot lines of Reality is *uniqueness*. Reality seeks more and more uniqueness.
- One of the plot lines of Reality is *transformation*. Reality seeks more and more transformation.

MY TRANSFORMATION IS THE TRANSFORMATION OF THE WHOLE

Now, get this sentence: **my transformation is the transformation of the whole.** When I'm transforming, it all lives in me. Soon we'll look deeper into what it means that *it all lives in me*, that's a particular level in a realization of self.

But it's true, right?

As Albert Einstein said, anyone who thinks they're separate from the whole is engaged in *an optical delusion of consciousness.*

So, it all lives in me.

- ◆ My transformation is the transformation of the whole.
- ◆ My Eros moves the Eros of the whole.
- ◆ My intimacy evolves the intimacy of the whole.

And that notion—that Reality is a Story—is not a made-up idea. It is not a made-up story.

It is rooted in the best of all the exterior and interior sciences.

There's an idea in the interior sciences that not only is my transformation part of the whole, but my transformation actually *causes* the transformation of the whole.

That's a very big idea. It's a very beautiful idea.

In the lineage of Solomon, there's something that's called The Great Gathering, the *Idra Rabba,* which changed the course of history and defined the Renaissance. There were eight people there, there were eight people there that actually transformed. And because they participated directly in the whole, and the whole participated in them, the whole thing changed.

So that's the *keymaster*. That's *story*. The last thing I'm interested in doing is making an intellectual point. It's making the key so precise that it can open the door.

So, we talked out the question *Where? Where am I?* I'm in the Intimate Universe. I live in the Intimate Universe.

We're now at the question *who? Who am I?*

The Intimate Universe lives in me, uniquely, which is why I can act on it.

If I was separate from it, alienated from it, I would have no effect on it. I'm hopeless. I can't find love in a hopeless place.

But if I'm actually *participatory*, I live in the Intimate Universe, and the Intimate Universe lives in me—ontologically, scientifically, interior science and exterior science—then, quite literally, just like one cell in the body impacts the entire body, **I am a cell in the superorganism, and I have a non-local effect on the entire organism.**

Of course! We're in the Field of Value.

IMAGINE HEALING THE GLOBAL INTIMACY DISORDER

We're going to go nine more steps. Again, not in order to get another piece of information, but because it's something else you need—I want you to have the *keys*. Each key is super simple.

1. We have global challenges.
2. Global challenges require global coordination.
3. Global coordination requires global resonance—we have to resonate with each other, or we can't coordinate.
4. Global resonance requires some level of global coherence. That's why no one got together after Covid to figure out what to do together—there's no coherence. So, global resonance requires global coherence.
5. Global coherence requires some form of global intimacy—just like in a couple, we need to be intimate with each other in some way, or we can't cohere.
6. The root of the meta-crisis is a global intimacy disorder.
7. Intimacy—in every relationship—is never based on the immediacy of arousal. Arousal is an interesting field, but intimacy is not based on that. Intimacy is based on a shared Story of Value.
8. You can trace every breakdown back to: *we don't have a shared Story of Value*—whether it is between a couple, in an organization, in a division, or between nations.
9. Meaning, the global intimacy disorder is based on the breakdown of a shared Story of Value.

What did we promise earlier? We were going to be Dr. House and do diagnostics. We have now done the diagnostic.

How do we restore intimacy and therefore respond to the meta-crisis? We create a **shared Story of Value**.

In order to do that, what do we need to do? **We need to show that value is real**.

That's what we've done at the think tank of the Center for World Philosophy and Religion[28]—and briefly touched upon here.

This hasn't been done anywhere in the world. That's what we've done.

Imagine that *exponentialized*. Who's willing to let our imagination run wild for a second? Just let it go unfettered. Unfettered imagination. Not pornographic imagination—bless the holy pornographic universe, which is not so holy. But let's go to the Erotic Universe, which is filled with arousal. The sexual cosmos, as my friend Howard Bloom calls it.[29]

Unbound. Untether your imagination.

Imagine all over the world, in any place in the world, that you can go to The Crossing. It's in China, it's in Malaysia, it's in the South, it's in the West, right? It's everywhere. You can just go for a weekend, and you just go to a Crossing weekend for three days and you get a sense of all this.

Imagine it's happening all over the world; it's waving through the world. It's happening in Beijing, and it's happening in Moscow, and it's happening everywhere. Wouldn't that be a different world, where we have taken a wildly profound step towards **healing the global intimacy disorder?**

Oh my God. Whatever happens, that's a big deal.

---

28   See David J. Temple, *Value is Real* (forthcoming, 2026), which is part of the Great Library, articulating a new Story of Value as a context for our diversity.

29   Howard Bloom, *The Case of the Sexual Cosmos: Everything You Know About Nature is Wrong* (2025).

CHAPTER SEVEN

SEPARATE SELF, TRUE SELF, AND EVOLUTIONARY UNIQUE SELF: THE THREE SELVES OF HOMO AMOR

THE THREE SELVES HAVE A RELATIONSHIP WITH THE PAST, PRESENT AND FUTURE

Our three great questions of CosmoErotic Humanism are:

- ◆ Who am I? Who are we?
- ◆ Where am I? Where are we?
- ◆ What's mine to do? What's ours to do? And what ought to be done?

We've talked about *where am I*, and we took a first dive into *who am I*.

Now, let's take a look at *Homo amor* Theory of Self.

Who am I? I'm a unique expression of the Intimate Universe. I'm *Homo amor*. I'm *the Universe: A Love Story* in person.

But I'm going to put that aside for now. We're going to start again in some sense. We've finished part one. We're just going to take a little dive, beginning part two, which is: **let's actually build the most robust, powerful vision of human identity, which will explode as the fourth Big Bang—as** *Homo amor.*

But let's start from the beginning.

So, we're going to talk about *three selves*. We will introduce the first self. The first self is the **psychological self.**

I'm now putting everything we talked about aside and just starting from the beginning again. I'm just going to begin a conversation. The large vision we just had about I am *Homo amor, the Universe: A Love Story* in person—we will get back to that. We just dropped that in the space.

We're going to step into this understanding, this realization that we've spent fifteen to twenty years on:

Who is *Homo amor*? **Who am I?**

We will talk about the three selves. One self is deeply related to the past, another self is deeply related to the present, and a third self is deeply related to the future.

Past, present, and future themselves are First Principles and First Values of the Cosmos. I have to be in right relationship to the past, in right relationship to the present, and in right relationship to the future.

- ◆ I can have a distorted relationship with the *past* or I can have a relationship with the past that is whole.
- ◆ I can have a distorted relationship with the *present* or a I can have a whole relationship with the present.
- ◆ I can have a distorted relationship with the *future* or I can have a full, powerful relationship with the future.

But past, present, and future themselves are First Principles and First Values of the Cosmos.

THE FIRST SELF: SEPARATE SELF, THE PSYCHOLOGICAL SELF

Now, the self that is called *Homo sapiens* is the psychological self. But remember, *Homo amor* is the fulfillment of *Homo sapiens*. So we're not going to leave *Homo sapiens* behind; we're going to take *Homo sapiens* with us.

The psychological self is *Homo sapiens*. Another word for the psychological self is the *separate self*. Another word for the psychological self is the *ego self*—and that's a legitimate, powerful self.

It's all of my history.

Now, what was the big move in consciousness or in thinking in the last 200 years?

In one dimension of self, the past *matters*. For example, imagine you're Freud, you're working for Breuer, you're in Vienna. You've got thousands of women in Vienna who are suffering from intense hysteria. They're all thought to be clinically insane or demented, or morally shattered in some way.

And Freud says, *No. Actually, they've been abused. Actually, there's a story in the past that has hijacked the present.*

And Freud challenges the entire nascent establishment of medicine and says, *We have to take the past seriously as a healing key.*

That's very powerful. That's not nothing. That's a huge realization.

The entire therapeutic movement of the Western world is rooted in the psychological self, in the past.

It's about the past of the individual, but it's also about recovering the notion that the past drives me.

My colleague Sam Harris will claim, *I'm only driven by my past; I can never make a free will decision in the present. Yesterday always determines today.*[30] That's one version of the psychological self. Therapy is another version of the psychological self. The psychological self basically says the past is a very big deal.

- Is the psychological self wrong? Of course not.
- Is the psychological self the *full* measure of self? Of course not.

So, I've got to take the past seriously. And by the way, when I say take the past seriously, I also mean I've got to take the past seriously *in the lineage of my family.*

But I've also got to take the past seriously in the broader sense that I get that **I am a direct product of the first three Big Bangs.** And I'm not just here as a separate self—I'm emergent from the whole thing. Without trees, I don't exist. Without yesterday and the entire evolutionary process, I'm not even a meaningful concept. There is nothing that exists independently of everything, which is this other realization: that all of the past lives in me.

My personal past, my lineage past, my cultural past, my psychological past, my cosmological past—that's all part of the psychological self.

But the focus today in the world on the psychological self is on *my personal story* and its yesterdays.

And here's the funny thing: it is true that you actually can't take the next steps without first taking that seriously.

And if you notice, I will never just deride something. I'll always say, *what's the truth in it?* **Everything's true but partial, and no one's smart enough**

---

30   This paraphrases Harris' view that free will is an illusion in the libertarian sense. According to Harris, all of our decisions are the product of prior causes—genetics, conditioning, neurobiology, and circumstance—over which we have no ultimate control. While he acknowledges that we feel like we make choices, he contends that we cannot choose what we will choose. Thus, our sense of authorship is not reflective of true freedom, but of deterministic processes unfolding within us.

to be entirely right or entirely wrong. So we've got to gather everything at the table and then reweave it into a whole.

Therapy is important.

But it's even deeper. In order to become *Homo amor*, we have to actually go back and recover the pieces of our personal story that somehow got split off.

So, in order to get to tomorrow, we have to first do at least one piece of work to become *Homo amor* within the realm of the psychological self.

Because my story is chapter and verse in the Universe: A Love Story. At the same time, it is important to understand that my work of psychological wholeness is not merely mine. So when I do that work of psychological wholeness *as Homo amor*, then I'm fixing the whole thing, I'm changing the whole thing.

Each piece is a key that opens a door—and it opens a precise love and a precise energy between all of us.

CHAPTER EIGHT

HOMO AMOR INJUNCTION FOUR: TAKE CARE OF UNFINISHED BUSINESS

SHAME BLOCKS EROS

So what do we actually need to do with the split-off parts of our stories as *Homo amor* to emerge the next step?

The fourth injunction is **to take care of unfinished business**. There is this sort of *cleaning up* that needs to happen. Osho, my first teacher, said we need to do some plumbing, you know, **to unplug the pipes of the past.**

We're going to do some cleaning up. We're going to take care of some unfinished business.

So, to enter into this topic, here's the sentence: **shame blocks Eros.**

That's the sentence. **Shame blocks Eros.**

Shame is not the experience that I did something wrong; what *Homo amor* understands is that shame is the experience that *I am wrong*.

Do you get the difference?

Shame is not the experience that I did something bad. Shame is the experience that I am bad.

In other words, I'm broken. The factory that made me, that could have replaced the bad parts, shut down long ago. Like an old model Ferrari, I'm not fixable. That's the experience of shame.

And shame is multi-layered and insidious. Meaning, you chop off the hydra of the snake of shame in one place, and it reappears in another place.

So, what is *the core* of shame?

So, what is our Eros equation?

> *Eros is radical aliveness desiring deeper contact and greater wholeness (which itself is value).*[31]

Eros Equation of CosmoErotic Humanism:

Eros is the experience of radical aliveness, desiring ever-deeper contact and ever-greater wholeness.

That's Eros. Reality is Eros. Eros lives in me.

So, imagine if my essential early experience of aliveness is that my aliveness itself is bad.

We are reformulating the conversation on shame in the frame of *Homo amor*. It's now a whole different conversation. So, in other words:

- ◆ Eros is aliveness.
- ◆ My aliveness is unique.
- ◆ If I go back, I realize that in the earliest dimensions of my life are hidden stories in which my very precise, gorgeous, unique aliveness was rejected.

And at the earliest stages of life, it's impossible to disambiguate, meaning to distinguish, to tell the difference, between my aliveness and my goodness.

Because aliveness is a value of Cosmos.

---

31   *Eros = Radical Aliveness x Desiring (Growing + Seeking) x Deeper Contact x Greater Wholeness x Self-Actualization/ Self-Transcendence (Creation [Destruction])*

And this step is very beautiful because it changes the shame conversation. **It changes how we engage and transform shame as *Homo amor*.** It means that **shame is alienation from my own aliveness, from my own Eros, from my own Value.**

Now, look what happens. It gets crazy now.

So, imagine you're a therapist, and you're doing great work in shame. The only thing is, you don't think that there's a Field of Value. Because that's a given in the post-modern therapeutic world: *there's no Field of Value; value is all made up—it's a psychological construct.*

And you're doing exercise after exercise to heal shame, and it doesn't get anywhere, as lots of shame-work doesn't, because **the experience of shame itself is that I'm alienated from the Field of Value.**

And my unique story is a unique fabric of the Field of Value.

So in order to become *Homo amor*, I need to re-access the Field of ErosValue by reclaiming the shamed or split-off parts of my story.

HOMO AMOR HEALS THE EXPERIENCE OF HER DESIRE AND NEEDS BEING SHAMEFUL

There's one more piece to this. It's crazy beautiful.

So, remember we talked about the birds in that beautiful murmuration. And what did we say? We said the birds are an example of simple first rules:

1. Stay close to your neighbor.
2. Don't fly too close.
3. Fly towards the center.

Three rules.

And we said that the movement of Reality towards meta-crisis is based on the three anti-value rules:

1. **We're in rivalrous conflict.** I'm measured against someone else.
2. **I have no value that's intrinsic in and of myself.** If I'm not commodifiable, or what we call "successful," I don't have value. And when someone's not successful by that commodifiable standard, what we say is, *Oh, but they're a very pure person.* Or, *But he's a very devoted husband.* In other words, *devotion, purity, sincerity*—those are booby prizes. We all know that, *actually, I'm not successful.* So, the second rule is **I have no intrinsic value.**
3. **My desire, the contours and the shape of my desire and my needs are in some sense shameful.** There's something about my desire that's wrong. There's something about my needs that's wrong. I can't quite identify it, but I know it's there. I can feel the shaming and the humiliation in trying to meet my core needs and desires.

That's the topography of shame through the new Story of Value called *Homo amor.*

So, our first step has to be to address this first level of shame.

WE DO THE *HOMO SAPIENS* INNER WORK AS *HOMO AMOR*

I want to leave you, as we tenderly close this chapter, with a couple of images.

The first image is one of the greatest cinematographic accomplishments of the late 20th and early 21st century. You've probably seen the movie called *A Beautiful Mind.* It's a story about a man who won a major prize in science. He has so much shame and so many demons. At some point, his demons enter him. But in the movie we think they are real people—we don't even realize that they're demons. We go with him on the journey.

He does this deep work on himself, he does every form of healing work he can imagine. And finally he's in this audience at Princeton. He's being given a prize. This is after he has done all the work on himself. And he walks out of the theater with his wife. And there are those three figures who have tormented him his whole life—these three figures of his shame.

And they're not gone.

But they don't have the steering wheel.

And he looks at them, and they look at him, and he kind of nods, and he goes on to create and to be.

Homo amor understands that we're always going to be doing inner work. We never leave the work of *Homo sapiens* behind, but it becomes *Homo amor* work.

So we're not just doing a shame exercise. Or we're not just doing breath work, or whatever healing modality we are in. And there's no "just" in either shame or breath work—they are both gorgeous and beautiful and sacred.

But we're actually entering through a different door.

We are *Homo amor.*

Shame blocks Eros.

Eros is the Field of Reality that lives in me.

When I begin to transform my shame, I'm not just doing *personal* work. In the same moment, I'm doing *political* work, *economic* work, *cosmic* work, and *mystical* work.

So you can feel *Homo amor* begins to enter.

Take a moment to sit in a moment of gentle silence.

Just to tenderly let *Homo amor* not just enter our minds, not just our hearts, but our whole selves, and the inside of ourselves, and the Field of Value that is ourselves.

And so it is.

And all obstacles are melted away.

And *Homo amor* begins to emerge.

Then listen once more to this beautiful song…

    ♪ *Michael row your boat ashore, hallelujah* ♪

We're rowing the boat ashore.

Hallelujah.

Amen.

CHAPTER NINE

HOMO AMOR INJUNCTION FIVE: TAKE THE RED PILL

DEMOCRATIZING THE HERO

I have been tracking a group of people that I've studied for the last 25 years out of pure admiration. It's a unit in the army known as Easy Company. Spielberg and Hanks created a series called *Band of Brothers* about these men. The reason I tracked them is that I am deeply drawn to the literature of heroes—in premodern, modern, and postmodern contexts. The hero.

Because the hero knows something. What does the hero know? **The hero is the person who's taking the red pill.**

In the movie *The Matrix*, human beings who are plugged into the matrix are slaves. They are used to power the world of the machines while believing they are living normal lives, which are, in fact, generated by the matrix. The matrix is the world of illusion. If you take the red pill, you become unplugged. You wake up from this illusion, and you step out of the prison into the larger truth of who you truly are.

The hero takes the red pill and wakes up in first-person.

A hero means that *I know I'm not separate from the whole. So I'm willing to lay down my life for the whole.* But even more dramatically, I *live* for the whole. That's the beginning of a first-person realization of *Homo amor.*

109

Heroes are early adopters of *Homo amor*.

The problem with heroes is they can die for false causes. So the heroes have to clarify their prism and actually know—what cause should I die for? **But even more powerfully, what cause should I live for?**

The democratization of the hero is the experience of Homo amor.

That's the core. I just wanted to briefly introduce this, just to feel it.

The truth is that—just like *I want to know what love is,* and I can trust my own desire to know as pointing towards the real—the truth is that in our innermost hearts, we want to be heroes. And we actually know that we are heroes. And we're not satisfied; **we don't recognize ourselves until we recognize ourselves as heroes.**

RECAPITULATION

So, in the first part of our conversation, we talked about "Where are we?" And we entered into not the poly-crisis, but the meta-crisis.

And the reason we're calling it the meta-crisis is because it's got an underlying root cause. Remember Dr. House—diagnosis. That's super hopeful, right? Because with the right diagnosis, we can actually address it.

So, we did a whole piece on the question, *Where are we?*

And then, we stepped into the response. In the response, we said that the only thing that changes history at a time between worlds and a time between stories is actually a new story. And we showed that story itself is not made up—that story is a First Principle and First Value of Cosmos.

Story exists all the way down the evolutionary chain.

Story exists all the way up the evolutionary chain.

And we said that **stories are ways that we create coherent complexity.**

Simple first rules. We saw the murmuration of the birds and the three rules:

- Fly close to your neighbor.
- Don't fly too close.
- Fly towards the center.

So, how do we create coherent complexity of 8 billion humans and—hold this sentence—emergent future galactic relationships?

Didn't you see *Avatar*? I'm not going to go down that road now. But a very close friend of mine is the leading researcher in this field. He has gathered more material on this than literally anyone else in the world. There's little doubt in my mind, as sure as I am, that we are not alone in the universe. The amount of information now on intelligence beyond Earth is overwhelming. It's not cute. It's not pop. It's the amount of *empirical evidence*. And in the last five years, this has gone from the periphery to the mainstream. So, virtually every mainstream legacy newspaper in the world—*The Guardian, New York Times,* in China, in Europe—everyone's written articles on validated information. That wasn't true five years ago. It's a very big deal.

So we need this coherent complexity to prevent 8 billion people from disappearing—but actually, it's an even bigger galactic story.

We need a shared Story of Value or we go extinct.

That's what we're talking about. *Homo amor* is that shared Story of Value.

We started with the question, *Where am I?* And we told the story of the Amorous Cosmos—and we alluded to it scientifically. *Where do I live?*

I live in an Amorous Cosmos, an Intimate Universe, a CosmoErotic Universe, in the Universe: A Love Story, which is governed by Eros equations and Intimacy equations, which govern the interior and

exterior sciences all the way down and all the way up the evolutionary chain.

That is a big story.

Then we moved from *Where am I?* to *Who am I?* and *who are we?*

THE SECOND SELF OF *HOMO AMOR*: TRUE SELF, THE MYSTICAL SELF

We said there are three selves that together make up *Homo amor*.

The first self is the psychological self. The psychological self is all about the past—therapy, trauma, shame. Psychological self, separate self, or ego self is gorgeous, beautiful, and important. It has a distorted, broken form, and it has a holy form. There's always a holy and a broken *hallelujah*.

The second self, the mystical self, usually ignores the first self. But *we have to put them together—they can't be in a fight with each other.*

We said, the mystical self, also known as True Self or eternal self, has three faces:

- ◆ **Third person:** We turn to the third-person world that is alive and realize it's all this dazzling dance of allurement—37.2 trillion cells in your body.
- ◆ **Second person:** The Infinite Intimate. We got lost and fell into the arms of the Infinite Intimate—not as a New Age practice, not as a fundamentalist practice, but as a direct realization of the direct experience of being held in the arms of She. And we realized that every word I speak is collected and heard by the Field of Intelligence. It was a direct realization.
- ◆ **First person.** We opened up the first-person hero, and we went deep into Sally Kempton's meditation.

We went into the world of the wild—the wild that steps out of the matrix. We had a direct realization, a direct experience of mystical self.

I just recapitulated the steps we took so we can see the thread. That was just a little love note, so we can see the thread and feel where we are.

THE THIRD SELF OF *HOMO AMOR*: FUTURE UNIQUE SELF

Now we're about to step into the third self.

The psychological self serves at the altar of the past. Beautifully. In a sacred way and in a broken way.

Mystical self serves at the altar of the present:

1. Whether it's the love right here in front of me and *I'm falling into your arms right now.*
2. Whether it's *Tat Tvam Asi,* Thou Art That. *I am part of the entire field.*
3. Whether it's the awareness of everything—as disclosed by mathematics and science and molecular biology, and all the schools of physics—happening right now in this second. So it's the demand of the present—the beauty of the present.

Each one of these has a light and a shadow side.

But now we move into this third self. Because *Homo amor* includes the best of psychological self and the best of mystical self, but *Homo amor* really begins to appear when we introduce the third dimension. And the third dimension is the future. **There is a future self.**

So, in order to find our way into this **future unique self,** we actually want to enter and just begin to touch it through an entirely different door.

CHAPTER TEN

HOMO AMOR INJUNCTION SIX:
LIVE YOUR STORY

BEYOND DEPRESSION & LONELINESS

So, do you know someone in your life who has experienced depression? Yes, right? Depression is real. There's this malaise of depression sweeping the world. In the pandemic of mental breakdowns, greater than we've seen at any other time, for all the reasons we've pointed towards, depression is at the core.

So, what's the etiology—which is a fancy word for the basic underlying structure? What animates depression? What is the motivational architecture of depression? What drives depression at its core? What drives it?

This is unimaginably important. If we cut through, **the etiology or the motivational architecture of depression is futility.** Futile, meaning it is not going to make a difference. It's futile. I actually don't make a difference. It doesn't really matter.

That's how Yuval Harari began: *It doesn't really matter whether I'm here or all of us are here*. That is a huge mistake. We pointed out what Harari was rebelling against—the holy heresy—but then it got completely lost.

So, **depression is replaceability.** It's a big sentence, right?

To be depressed is to be replaceable.

Depression is replaceability.

It doesn't matter. I'm trying to make a difference, so I participate in the rivalrous conflict, which is one of those anti-value simple first rules. I do *rivalrous conflict* in order to stand out—which is the second simple rule— to give myself an illusion of being valuable. But the only thing I really feel about myself is my desire, but—the third rule—everyone tells me my desire is kind of corrupt and fucked up. It's quite depressing. I don't actually feel like I matter.

I'm made up of matter, but I don't realize that I'm made up of *what matters*—and that **my *what matters* matters infinitely**. I can't get access to that because the mainstream legacy institutions are telling me that it's not true.

In parentheses, the overwhelming majority of therapists worldwide subscribe to the hierarchical position that we started with. That's just true in the Western world, and for many reasons. There is substantial data supporting this—not in terms of that particular quote, but in terms of the general opinion structures.

So in therapy, you're talking to someone who essentially believes that meaning is made up and that value is contrived, in which case you can't have any intrinsic meaning. How well is that going to go? As my friend Diana used to say, *good luck with that!*

Wow, that's a big deal.

And then the next step is, I start to get lonely. On the one hand, I'm depressed. On the other hand, I'm lonely.

Now, here's the paradox. It's very subtle. It's very beautiful.

Loneliness is telling me something precisely the opposite to what depression tells me.

- **Depression** says I'm replaceable—futility.
- But **loneliness** is this inexorable, this unavoidable feeling that

there's something about me that I want to share.

There's something about me that's actually important and that actually deserves sharing. It so deserves sharing that it's actually a tragic experience if I'm unable to share it. It's so tragic that I can be "successful" in the context of rivalrous conflict governed by win-lose metrics, but *if I'm fundamentally lonely, I feel devastated, broken, empty, filled with malaise, and suicidal.*

Suicide rates are going way up. For every suicide, there are about five to ten times more *attempted* suicides—that means people brave enough to make the attempt. And then there are exponentially more people just thinking about suicide all over the world because they're lonely.

But loneliness is actually telling me something important.

In Great Britain, they actually appointed a ministry of loneliness. For the first time, there's actually a ministry that deals with loneliness. In six or seven countries around the world today there are ministries of loneliness. Loneliness is this epidemic that is just devastating people.

But loneliness is actually pointing to something. Loneliness points to my singularity. **Singularity means my uniqueness.**

My experience of loneliness is actually a whisper from Cosmos that says there's something irreducibly beautiful and unique that deserves to be experienced. And there's a story that I'm living that deserves to be told.

It is not just that I want to tell you about my psychological self, although there's a dimension of that.

It is not just that I am leaving my story behind in this kind of classical, mystical self: *I'm fully present in the now, there's no story.*

It's actually this deeper realization that *my story matters*—that it matters infinitely.

HOMO AMOR INJUNCTION SIX: LIVE YOUR STORY

"Your story matters" was our third injunction. And because my story matters infinitely, **the sixth injunction in becoming *Homo amor* is: live your story**.

But you can't live your story unless you can *tell* your story. Because I have to be able to *see* my story and know: ***I'm the hero of my own story***. And I have to know that my story matters in this insane way.

There's a story in West Africa, which is one of my favorite stories. When I wanted to teach my son Zion how to read, we read this story. So we read this story probably like a hundred times. This was his learning-how-to-read story. He never wanted to read it again. If I ever mention it, he kind of looks at me with a baleful killer glance.

But it's a beautiful story. It's about this West African tribe.

> There's a West African lineage tradition that is starving. And then, somehow, in the middle of their starvation, they organize this great prayer. And then this figure—this beautiful maiden from the heavens, in this story—comes and places this vat of milk in the center of the town.
>
> The elders, of course, are thrilled: we've solved the hunger problem. Let's move on.
>
> But this young man, he hears that there's a vat of milk. And he hears that there's some beautiful maiden. Everyone says, "You're not allowed to look," but he's got to be able to see her.
>
> So he hides behind the bush, and he sees her, and he's smitten.
>
> And although Greek and Roman literature didn't apply there, Cupid's arrow went into his heart right there in West Africa.

And he jumps out from behind the bush, and he "seizes her wrist"—which by the way is not generally a good way to do a marriage proposal post-MeToo, although it probably wasn't that good before, either.

But he seizes her wrist, and he says, "You must marry me."

And she actually looks at him, and she says, "Yes, on one condition."

"What's the condition?"

"I've got to go back to heaven—to my heavens. I'm going to bring something with me. Then I'm going to give you one condition, if you fulfill that condition, I'm with you forever."

She goes back to heaven. She comes back, as always happens in West African legends, with a box—there's always a box.

And she says, "If you open this box, I may have to leave you."

He says, "Of course, I'm not going to open the box. My mother would say, am I out of my mind? I've got the girl."

They put the box under the bed.

Then they have one child, then two children, and they have three children. They're ecstatic. They're happy. It's gorgeous, you know?

And she sometimes takes trips, and he sometimes takes trips. But whenever she takes a trip, he's dying to see what's in the box. He's just dying.

Like, "What is in the box?"

But he's like, "I can't do that."

So now, we're 17 years into the marriage, and she's away. And she comes home. And women, when they're away, always know what men did when they were home alone. Keep that in mind, my friends.

She says, "You opened the box."

He said, "How did you know I opened the box?"

And she's just waiting with bated breath, and she says, "What did you see?"

He says, "I don't understand. I opened it. There was nothing there."

And she says, "I have to leave."

He says, "Why?"

She says "I went to the heavens, to the deepest place, and in that box was everything that was precious to me. But you looked, and for you, it was empty. So I can't stay."

So we have a box and in that box is everything that is precious to us.

But it's not just our psychological self.

It's our unseen future self. We are unseen future kings. We're royalty.

- It's all of my future memories.
- It's all of my dreams.
- It's all of my hero.
- It's all of my gorgeousness.
- It's all of my pathology.
- It's all of my fears.
- It's all of my trauma.
- It's everything that's me.

Past, present, and future.

It's that me that is not just an accident, but that was *intended* by all of Reality—that has a story that is infinitely valuable. My story matters. And it's that story that *needs* to be lived. And I'm desperate to live that story.

I'm desperate to live that story.

I'm not desperate to live that story just because it's *a social construction*. I'm desperate to live that story because my story is real—and story is a core structure of Cosmos.

This is big. And if you get this, it's one of those keys that just overturns the world.

How many people have read an article someplace, somewhere, where they say that the purpose of something was survival: *it was a survival mechanism*, it was an *evolutionary survival mechanism*? Who has read that word someplace, somewhere? It's just in the culture. It's just always there. *Oh, yes, yes. The prehistoric men and women—they loved music. Ah, but it was a survival mechanism. Oh, they would begin to pray. Yes, yes. It would coalesce people. It was a survival mechanism.*

But that's actually a deceit. What does a survival mechanism mean? What do the words mean? It means *I want to survive*.

And what does *I want to survive* mean? It means I want to live.

So what does survival mean? That life matters.

So, the mechanics of Cosmos would mean that if I'm broken, I die: *I'm broken. I don't fix myself.* But the notion that I fix myself, that I turn the world upside down in order to perpetuate, not just life in general, but *my life*—why? Because I'm crazy? Because there's some mechanical system? No!

Because the value of Cosmos is life; the value of Cosmos is *unique* life. Life is an inherent value structure of Cosmos.

What do most people spend most of their time thinking about? What do you spend most of your time thinking about? Yourself. All the time. That's what you're thinking about. *Sorry. Didn't want to disclose that.*

But what most people spend most of their time thinking about is their self: *my life story. How's it going? How's it not going? What's happening? Where's it going?*

Is that because we are obsessive narcissists? Is this the pathological narcissist society?

In some sense, that's the weakness of just mystical self. Because mystical self teachers all over the world tell you that you're trapped in this mind that keeps thinking about yourself, and that you should just get out of it and *move beyond your story*, because they identify "story" with psychological self. But story is not just psychological self.

So no, the reason you're thinking about yourself all the time is not because you're a pathological narcissist—not in the slightest.

So why are we thinking about ourselves all the time? Because we're eavesdropping on God thinking about us.

I'm listening in. I have a currency that allows me to listen in to the Universe's thoughts. The Infinite Intimate, the Universe, which intended me.

And by the way, that's just a very simple idea. It has got nothing to do with faith, nothing to do with dogma, nothing to do with New Age.

I was talking to someone a couple months ago, a dear friend of mine. And this person said to me, "Well, I'm done." I said, "What do you mean you're done?" He said, "Well, it's my life. I'm done." So I asked this dear friend, I said, "Well, *why* is it your life?"

It's kind of a shocking question, but why would you think it's your life?

- Oh, you decided when to be born? When did you make that decision?
- Oh, you decided where to be born? That's so interesting. Do you remember making that decision?
- You decided what kind of family to be born into? At least you made that decision, right? Nope.
- You decided what kind of intelligence to have?
- You decided what gender to have?
- You decided what kind of body type to have?

What did you actually decide? **No, I was intended by Reality. Reality intended me.** When you can actually feel that in your body—feel it in your body, *Reality intended me*—you have an immediate flash of awakening.

I was intended by Reality.

And when I'm thinking about myself all the time, it's not that I'm obsessed. *Yes,* there are some thoughts and patterns of thoughts I should probably liberate. And obviously, a mystical self has really important things to say in all of its three faces.

But at its core, *when I'm thinking about myself, I'm overhearing the divine conversation.*

So loneliness is a big deal.

Loneliness is the first opening to the realization that my story matters and I have to live that story.

So we just took the biggest pathological malaise in culture—loneliness—and we realized that it was actually a glimmer of this new Story of Value.

So we engage loneliness not just as the psychological self of *Homo amor;* we engage loneliness as the beginning of Unique Self.

Loneliness means there's a story that I have to live.

If you get this next sentence, ten things will light up like a pinball machine.

So loneliness means I have a story to live and the story matters.

And remember what we said?

There's a structure called Story in Cosmos.

What does story mean? Story means that there is a plot line. That it's going somewhere. That it's animated by desire and **it's animated by desire for a future.**

My future matters. You're right to be thinking about the future all the time—just not only *my* future, but *my future as part of the larger future.* Not a larger future in a way that obliterates me, but **I'm going to enter the larger future through my irreducibly unique story that matters infinitely.**

Now, had we not started it this way—although that would be lovely—we'd be in a completely different conversation. We could have started right here. But now, **when we enter this conversation, we're entering as Homo amor.**

So now, we have psychological self, mystical self, and what we call Unique Self. Another name for Unique Self is Future Self, or Evolutionary Unique Self.

Put them aside for now, though. We will play with that later.

Let's first be a little bit more in the energy of mystical self—just so you can feel the difference in the quality.

Because *Homo amor* is the most powerful version of psychological self.

And *Homo amor* does shame work at an entirely different level. At the Mystery School in 2022, we did a whole day on shame.[32] Shame is a deep thing. We've done this deep *dharma* on shame and how we take shame to the next level. We actually finished an 80,000-word volume on shame.[33] Brené Brown's work of telling your story of shame is the first level. It doesn't get you home, but it's necessary. But *the four levels of shame* is its own world.

So again, psychological self is wildly important—and we just tasted it.

Then we did this deep dive into the second face of *Homo amor*, which is mystical self. We looked at the three expressions of that mystical self: first-person, second-person, and third-person.

---

32 See *The Radical Path to the Transformation of Shame* in Marc Gafni, *From the CosmoErotic Universe to CosmoErotic Humanism: Why Is There Something Rather than Nothing* (2025).

33 Marc Gafni and Kristina Kincaid, *The Phenomenology of Eros, Volume 2* (forthcoming).

Now I want to just taste a little bit more of the feeling of mystical self before we plunge into the next step.

CHAPTER ELEVEN

HOMO AMOR SECOND SELF: INVOKING MYSTICAL SELF

MEDITATION FROM SALLY KEMPTON

We start with a meditation, in Sally Kempton's words.[34]

Sit in your comfortable upright posture, feeling the heaviness of your buttocks and thighs against the seat. With the breath, let your hips and thighs and sitting bones ground, and let your inner spine rise up from this grounded base, straight up through the crown of the head. With your awareness, follow the breath as it flows in and out.

And begin to feel that the breath is flowing in and out from the inner heart, the center behind the breastbone. As the breath flows in, it flows into the heart space. As the breath flows out, the inner heart space opens and expands.

With every breath, you let your awareness settle more deeply into the heart. Allowing the breath to caress and open the space of the heart. Allowing your attention to move very slowly, very mindfully through the cave of your own heart.

Exploring the energy there. Letting yourself feel more and more at home, more and more at rest inside the heart. As you rest easily in the heart, ask yourself the question, who am I?

---

34   Sally Kempton was a beloved teacher and spiritual practitioner who collaborated with Dr. Marc Gafni for many years. She was closely affiliated with the Center for World Philosophy and Religion. Sally passed away in 2023 and is deeply missed.

Ask the question and then notice what it is that arises in response. Remember, you're not looking for an answer in words. If words arise, ask, to whom do these words arise?

Who is this "I" who is aware of words and thoughts arising? If a feeling comes up, ask yourself, to whom does this feeling occur? Who am I?

What is this "I?" Each time you ask the question, pause and attend to whatever it is that arises in response. Each time you ask the question, attend to the spaciousness behind all words.

If a thought comes up, ask, who's having this thought?

Who is this "I?" Who am I?

As the question becomes a real inquiry, you may find that its form changes. From who am I? it might shift to, what am I?

Or what is this feeling of being me? Resting in the heart, stay with the inquiry. Asking the question, then attending to the spaciousness, the sense of presence that may arise in response.

Ask, and then wait. You're looking for that which is beyond all objects of awareness. You're looking for awareness itself.

Who am I? What is the "I"? Who am I?

We invoked my dear, beloved Sally Kempton in sharing her meditation. Sally used to tell me this joke:

So, a man comes to his psychiatrist and says, "I've got this real problem. I live in Los Angeles, but I know they've set this thing up. I know it's not really there. There's no real Los Angeles, right? But they've set it up, right? I'm going crazy. Like, the whole thing is set up, right?"

And the psychiatrist talks to him and says, "You know what? I've got a solution. Just tell your family you've got to go for a while, and go to Chicago. And you'll see that Chicago is there. So you'll realize it's not set up."

So the guy goes to Chicago, calls his psychiatrist, and says, "I'm telling you, they set Chicago up. For sure! Yeah, yeah, yeah, yeah. They set Chicago up. Oh, God."

And so the psychiatrist says, "Well, yeah, maybe your wife called ahead or something like that," trying to humor him, and says, "Okay, you know what you're going do? Do like this, okay? Don't tell anybody. Just go to Miami, but don't tell anyone you're going, so they don't have time to set it up. If you get there and it's there, then we're good."

So the guy's loves his psychiatrist. Brilliant, right? It's just insightful. Brilliant.

So the guy is really happy and he goes out the door.

The psychiatrist picks up the phone and says, "Set up Miami."

That's mystical self. Meaning, in a way, you have to actually get: *it is not really there.* Like that. It's powerful, right?

MYSTICAL SELF REALIZES THERE'S A LARGER FIELD OF VALUE

So we got piece one. That's one.

So now, two, which is just another snapshot of mystical self.

So, Heath Ledgers made a movie called Batman. So let's take a look at Batman for a moment.

We're in mystical self. We're just setting the ground for Unique Self and Future Self, but first, we just want to get the taste of mystical self and why it matters.

So mystical self tells me: *It's not as real as you think. You can get underneath it. There's an illusion, and you need to penetrate that illusion.*

So that's one dimension of mystical self. By itself, that can be pathologized—but it's a realization. There's something there.

But there's a second realization of mystical self.

So let's go to the movies. Here's a short clip.

Movie Scene Description – *The Dark Knight*

In a tense moral showdown orchestrated by the Joker, two ferries—one filled with civilians, the other with prisoners—are rigged with explosives. Each boat is given a detonator to the other's bomb, and the chilling ultimatum is delivered: blow up the other ferry or risk being blown up yourselves. As panic sets in, passengers on both boats struggle with the ethical weight of the decision. Tensions rise, votes are cast, and fear threatens to override decency. In the end, both groups are faced with a defining question: will they choose self-preservation—or moral courage?

What happens is that neither side—not one person—is willing to do it, to blow up the other ferry. It's an incredible scene. And the Joker then goes insane because the joke is on him.

All of a sudden, we hear this crazy laughter that is deeper than the Joker's laughter. **It's the laughter that holds paradox.** It's the laughter that cuts through Reality—to its very essence.

The clock hits 12. Not one person is willing to not be a hero on both boats. That is the direct realization of Mystical Self. If I'm only a separate self in rivalrous conflict, is there any chance that there's not going to be at least one person in both boats who will press the detonator?

This was Heath Ledger's last movie. He died right afterward.

But what the Joker basically says is, *there's no one who's actually not involved in some form of rivalrous conflict. And that's what's driving everything.* So he takes the police commissioner in town, who seems to be a hero standing for the good, and turns him into a villain. Everything is turned upside down. There is no Field of Value. That's the Joker's point. And now, he's going to make that point clear in public.

But then, the divine laughter of Cosmos overturns the whole thing. And the Joker goes insane. He was wrong. There is a Field of Value.

Mystical Self is the hero who realizes there's a larger field.

And if there's nothing in the world—in the Field of Value—that I'm willing to die for, then I'm already dead. If what I'm willing to die for is only my egocentric family, then I'm also already dead. That's just an egoic extension of myself.

There is a larger field. That's the realization of Mystical Self.

CHAPTER TWELVE

HOMO AMOR SELF THREE: INVOKING FUTURE SELF, EVOLUTIONARY UNIQUE SELF

YOUR UNIQUENESS WAS INTENDED BY COSMOS

Now we go to Unique Self. We go to Future Self. We go to Evolutionary Unique Self.

And what Future Self and Unique Self say is:

If I was willing to die for it as mystical self,
I'm willing to live for it as Unique Self.

That's the whole move.

This is where *Homo amor* is born.

Homo amor is not just separate self, not just personality, and not just psychological self.

But it is also not just mystical self in mad intimate communion with the Infinity of Intimacy knowing that *I am personally addressed*. I'm not just in the field of mystical self, although that's true. That is why a monk can light themselves on fire protesting the Vietnam War—and of course, no one is to light themselves on fire; that's not the point.

The point is *I feel the larger field, but now I've got to step back into life.*

And to step back into life, I've got to go to the third self. So the third self is what we are calling Unique Self.

Psychological self is the first of the three selves. Psychological self is separate self. Separate self is what we call *personality.* That's the personal in the sense that it's my personality.

- It's my stuff.
- It's my trauma.
- It's my fears.
- It's my hopes.
- It's my dreams.
- It's my separate self stuff.

That's what we call the first-level story.

That's what we usually call story. It can have my victim story. It can have my decent story. It's all that stuff. And it's beautiful. I do the deep work there, and it's gorgeous, and I can have a healthy or broken *hallelujah.*

Then I go to mystical self, and I realize *I'm not just my personality*. My "I" is actually the entire field, and I'm personally addressed by the Infinity of Intimacy that knows my name. I take the red pill. I open up. I explode. I realize all the laws of chemistry that are happening in every second.

You know that phrase in English—*there's chemistry* between people? And people think it's a cute phrase. It's not cute. What does chemistry mean? We use words, but *what is chemistry*? Science people—what is chemistry?

Chemistry is the allurement between separate parts. There are valences of electrons, and the allurement between separate parts creates new configurations of intimacy, which we call new chemical compounds.

That's chemistry. We literally forget that it's the same thing all the way up and all the way down the evolutionary chain.

And when we say there is *chemistry between us,* of course, it's not *exactly* the same structure; there is an evolution of chemistry, but it's the precisely same idea. That's what we mean when we say that Divinity wakes up in us as the "third-person."

It's all chemistry. It's all allurement. It's all alive.

So mystical self is this level *beyond* my personality.

Then I go to the third level and I get to Unique Self. And at Unique Self, I'm *in the personal* again.[35]

That is the shock, right? I was in this impersonal field, in this *seamless coat of the Universe*, and then **I realized that the seamless coat of the Universe was seamless, but it wasn't featureless.**

And *I am its unique feature.* Not because I'm a separate self, not because I'm an unintended accidental personality, but because **my uniqueness was intended by Cosmos, and my story was intended by Cosmos.**

WE REACH FOR UNIQUE SELF IN AN EVOLUTIONARY CONTEXT

I just want you to *feel it* for a second, and then we'll jump forward.

If I'm a **separate self,** I'm a puzzle piece. I'm separate, trying to find a puzzle—but everyone tells me there is no puzzle. That's a little crazy-making, right?

If I'm **True Self,** I have no puzzle piece. *That separate thing is just an illusion.* Albert Einstein said, *separation is an optical delusion of consciousness;*[36] *there's just one whole.* **There's just the whole puzzle—there are no puzzle pieces.**

---

35 For a deeper understanding of Unique Self, see Marc Gafni, *Awakening Your Unique Self: The Radical Path to Personal Enlightenment* (2014).

36 Albert Einstein, in a 1950 letter to Rabbi Robert S. Marcus, referred to separation as "an optical delusion of consciousness," emphasizing the need to widen our circle of compassion.

But that's also crazy-making, because here I am thinking about myself, which we said before is *eavesdropping on the mind of God.*

So I get to Unique Self, and now I'm a puzzle piece that actually completes the puzzle. It's a shocking realization.

I'm a unique puzzle piece. And it's only my unique puzzle piece that completes the whole.

There is no whole without my unique puzzle piece. That's the beginning of Unique Self. But it's more than that.

I'm Unique Self in an evolutionary context. So, what's an evolutionary context? What does evolution mean? **Evolution is a series of transformations.** So evolution means I'm reaching for more. Evolution means I desire more. I desire more value. There's more to come. That's what evolution means: *there's more to come.*

It's not like there's God or Value that is *unchanging.* There's more God to come. There's more value to come.

And where does the *more God to come* or *more value to come* come from? Ontologically, structurally, in the world—where does it come from? *You!*

Who am I? Who are you?

You are an irreducibly unique expression of the Field of ErosValue that is the initiating, the starting energy of all that is, that lives in you, as you, and through you, that never was, is, or will be ever again other than through you.

And as such, you're a unique quality of Eros. And you're a unique quality of value. And you're a unique quality of intimacy. And you're a unique godding that never was, is, or will be ever again in the world.

136

And as such, you have the capacity to transform and involve the entire thing by being the fullest self that you are. Which you can only do if you clarify and embrace the utter fullness of your unique desire.

Because Reality is Eros, and Eros is desire. And desire lives uniquely in me and my unique desire isn't only physical—although it's also embodied.

But as Buddha said, *have few desires, but have great ones.*

It is about the question *what is my deepest heart's desire?*

My deepest heart's desire is the desire of evolution, awake and alive in me.

It pulls for the future. Reality wants something for me.

It's not just my future desire. It's not just that's who I am. It's not just that's how Reality is structured.

Reality *needs* me.

You cannot experience yourself as welcome in the Universe unless you realize that you are uniquely needed by the Universe for something which is heroic and large and dramatic and wondrous.

And as long as I'm thinking small, as long as I'm playing a small game, I feel alienated from my own life. And I feel this sense of shame because there's a *good* sense of shame.

See, what we do is we shame *shame.*

On the first level, we do say that shame is terrible: *let's tell the story of our shame and get beyond our shame.* But you have to be careful because the principle of Tantra is non-rejection. Nothing is there by accident.

So, we can't *shame* shame. Do you get that? You can't shame *shame*. Shame must have a role here in this story; shame can't be only bad.

So, there's another level of shame, which is that we feel this shame because:

- ♦ We're not living our greatness.
- ♦ We're not living our full story.
- ♦ We're not living the full wonder of who we are, because we've compromised so many times, because we've given up so many dreams.

We've made our house so small. We were living in a mansion and then this room was unacceptable to my father so I shut that room down, and then this room didn't work for my social circle and I shut that room down, and then this room would have required too much from me, I would have had to feel too much so I shut that room down, and then this room needed me to kind of step up in a way that I was too uncomfortable and I wanted to be comfortable and I shut that room down. So I start with this mansion but then I'm living in a bad neighborhood in a little two-room flat with no running water. It doesn't matter how big it is, I've shut all the rooms down, so I'm *shamed.*

I'm shamed because I'm not being myself.

Who can find that in themselves?

Wow, that's big.

That's *Homo amor.*

> *Homo amor is Future Self. Homo amor is the call of the future. And it's the realization that Reality needs my service.*

Superman has good days and bad days. But Superman is not too depressed because Superman is pretty needed.

And it was couple of kids who came out of the lineage of Solomon, that were sitting around in Cleveland, Ohio, in the 30s and started writing these superhero comic books. That's what they did.

In the entire world of post-modernity, we've got this complete breakdown of everything, and then we got Marvel comics and Marvel movies all over the place.

Why?

Because they are about *heroes*!

VALENCE, VALOR, VALIENT, VALENCIA, VALUE

So we talked about chemistry. Chemistry is this movement towards Eros, towards creating larger intimacies. We call it *bonding*. There's this kind of chemical joining.

One of the qualities of a chemical element is its **valence.** So valence is the particular number of electrons that tells you how many electrons are missing or present—so it tells you how intimacy or allurement happens. That's valence.

Then we have a hero. And the hero is filled with **valor**. I'm playing with Latin now. What is valor? Heroic. Strong. Valor.

In America, we grew up on comic books, so there's this coming book called Prince Valiant Comics. Have you heard of Prince Valiant?

- ◆ We have **valence**, which is the way that I join.
- ◆ We have **valor**, the hero is valor.
- ◆ We have **valiant**, I'm a *valiant* hero.

And the root word is **valeria** or **valencia** in Latin, which means *be strong because you are value.*

The word in English is **value**, which is the only thing that can **validate** me.

You see the play? It's beautiful. It's just *right there.*

And it's my only **validity**, which gives me the experience that my life is wildly awake, alive, and worthy—because I'm a hero.

And a hero means I've got this radical, wild gift to give to the future that no one else but me can give.

And I promise you that that is so much more effective than any pharmacological intervention of any kind in depression. And *I mean that quite seriously.* **We're literally medicalizing the meaning-crisis.**

We have a crisis of value, which causes a meta-crisis.

WE HAVE AN ATTENTION CRISIS BECAUSE OUR KIDS BELIEVE: IT DOESN'T MATTER

And then part of the strategy of denial is that we medicalize it, just like we do with our kids. We have an *attention crisis* because we've told our kids *there's no value.* So they *don't want to* pay attention—because you only pay attention to what matters. And then we tell them, *oh, you've got ADHD.*

I've spent the last seven weeks going over probably 40–50 studies of ADHD. There are multiple factorial things at play, but essentially, what ADHD is at its core is *not* that they can't pay attention. The kids who have ADHD are sitting, playing video games, *paying attention an entire day* tracking a video game.

It's not that they *can't* pay attention. They pay attention completely fine.

It's that they're *not interested* in paying attention to what we're telling them to pay attention to—because we told them that it didn't matter.

And then we're surprised that they're not paying attention. And then we punish them by medicalizing them. We drug them in order to make sure that they pay attention so they can work in the workforce—so they can fit into the rivalrous conflict win-lose metrics. And if they don't fit in, we tell them they're sick.

Do you understand that? We're destroying a generation of children.

EVERY SOCIETY IS BUILT ON THE TRANSMISSION OF VALUES BETWEEN GENERATIONS

Literally, we've lost the entire teacher-student relationship.

Every society is built on the transmission of value from one generation to the next.

That transmission of value is where we tell our children: *This is the real business of living. This is True. This is what it's about. We're not sure about this and that detail, but this—this is what it's about.*

We have literally broken the chain of transmission in generations.

TikTok has interrupted the transmission between generations.

Social media has interrupted the transmission between generations.

The internet is the exteriorization of the postmodern mind.

The postmodern mind says: *There's no story; there's no storyline. It's all just made up. There's no plotline to follow.* And the exterior expression of that frame is called the internet and social media.

And then, when our kids can't pay attention—because there's nothing to pay attention to—we medicalize them.

It's like, *wow!*

MY FUTURE SELF IS CALLING

So, I have to reclaim self on every level. We start with psychological self, but even more deeply, the psychological self goes into mystical self, which goes into Unique Self, which becomes *Homo amor.*

And *Homo amor* knows:

- ◆ I'm an irreducible unique expression of value.
- ◆ My future self is writing me a letter.
- ◆ My future self wants something from me.

I'm going to use a radical, shocking, weird expression, but I don't mean it the way you might hear it. But I want to use it and say it in the shocking way anyways because it's true.

My future self is the voice of God.

That's what we used to call the voice of God, the divine whisper, the whisper of *She*, the invitation of the Intimate Universe. It's the valence of Reality, it's the intention of Reality that calls me.

Now, remember, *the god you don't believe in doesn't exist.* We got that already. It's not *that* god. The god you don't believe in, I don't believe in. **But it's the Field of the Infinite Intimate that intends me and desperately needs me.**

And here's the story:

If you do not experience yourself as Homo amor, as being desperately needed by Cosmos, you are alienated from your own true nature, and you will break down medically, physically, emotionally, and psychologically.

All of the interventions will help in very temporary and partial ways, but it can't be fixed because you're basically rearranging the chairs on the decks of the Titanic.

It won't work—no chance, zero—because it's in violation of the nature of Reality.

But then all of a sudden, I experience myself as I truly am. And I'm desperately needed—desperately and personally.

You are personally needed because there's no way that I can do what you can do. I can't do it. No matter how hard I try. No matter how little hours of sleep I do. No matter how hard I work. No matter how hard I try and put it all together. There's some way of being and gifting that belongs to you and there's nothing that I can do to do that. Nothing.

And here's the last sentence…

You fucked up your life if you don't work this out. And no one is going to tell you that because you're not allowed to tell people they fucked up their lives. That's completely rude and inappropriate and terrible and politically incorrect and unliberal. But it's true.

It's not true that you can live any life you want and that there's no distinction between which life you choose.

That's absurd. That's utterly absurd and we all know it's absurd. We go to our therapist to tell us that it's not absurd—but it *is* absurd.

The very notion of Unique Self means that there's a gift that I can give.

- There's a life that I can live.
- There's a poem that I can write.
- There's a song that I can sing.
- There's a way of being, laughing, loving, living in the world that's mine and uniquely mine that's desperately needed by All-That-Is.

If it *only* serves me in my immediate circle,—it might be an egocentric scam. Now, of course you should serve in your immediate circle. For example, someone told me she learned how to cut hair so she could cut hair in her family, which I thought was stunningly beautiful. I moved to a small town in Vermont, because my son's mother got very sick, and I was afraid she wouldn't be able to take care of him. So, I wanted to live near her. I moved to a part of the world that I don't like. I hate the cold. But it was exactly the place that he needed me to be at that time, so it overrode everything else. He was ecstatic, and we created a great room for him in our house. He stayed with us for a year, and when his mom got better, he went back. Meanwhile, I'm still stuck in this place, and here we are in Vermont, right? Yet, I'm thrilled that I did it. It wasn't even a question. It's my son. We don't bypass biological family; we don't bypass our immediate circle.

That mad love we have for immediate circle and our biological family is not insignificant, but our family is so much bigger.

Our evolutionary family is so much bigger and it requires equal commitment. That's a shocking idea and we know it's true.

That's the nature of this *Homo amor* moment. We won't make it through based on a bunch of priests or rabbis or imams or subtle speculative minds or elite masters or isolated heroes. **We have to democratize the hero.**

We've got to become *Homo amor* together. We reorient the whole system.

A whale has value not because of whale oil. A whale has value because a whale is wildly gorgeous and beautiful.

PRACTICES OF HOMO AMOR

So the *Homo amor* question is, what does She want from me? Or what does He want from me? **What does Reality want from me?**

But more than *want*, **what does Reality *desperately need* from me?**

It's most valuable to try and clarify that, to know that, and to listen to the whisperings and be able to hear them.

> *Homo Amor Practice 1:*
>
> *Take a moment to write down and reflect on any thoughts that emerged for you, some insight that you had, or something that moved you.*
>
> *What moved you, or what opened you, or what provoked you?*
>
> *What does this mean for me?*
>
> *What would this mean—to open to this?*

If I can just ask one thing, please—like pretty-please-with-sugar-on-top-and-two-cherries? Be brave. Be courageous.

> *Homo Amor Practice 2:*
>
> *As a culture, we all have our different pathologies.*
>
> *Which social norms hold back my uniqueness?*

Now, just before you start, a word about social norms. It's not like we're against social norms. In a way, we're creating new social norms that belong to *Homo amor* that are based on these cosmic First Principles.

So we're not anarchists in that sense. Social norms always have a purpose. But which ones have outgrown their use with you and are simply holding back your unique flavor being expressed in the world, for the sake of the world?

The move of *Homo amor* is precisely the move from being *a spectator to time and existence*—as the Greeks wrote—to being a player. You're on the court, you're in the game, you're on the field.

I'm on the field. I'm not going to leave.

I'm a player. We're players.

That's where we're going.

There's a field. The field is one.One field.

It's a Field of Value. It's a Field of ErosValue.

It's an Amorous Cosmos.

That's where we are.

Who am I?

- I'm an irreducibly unique pattern of intimacy.
- I'm an irreducibly unique expression of ErosValue.
- There is a swing that's mine to take.
- The world desperately needs me to take it.

We are landing the Crossing now.

We're on the field.

We're trying to understand **what steps we need to take to cross over to the other side.**

Let's take a look at this clip from the movie *Bagger Vance*.

JOY COMES FROM TAKING YOUR SHOT FOR THE SAKE OF THE WHOLE: THE LEGEND OF BAGGER VANCE

In this scene from *The Legend of Bagger Vance*, Bagger guides Juna on the golf course, helping him feel the field.

Bagger Vance: *I think it's time.*

Juna: *Time for what?*

Bagger Vance: *Time for you to see the field.*

Juna: *I see the field. It's 445 yards long. It's got a little red flag at the end of it. It's 12 strokes ahead of me.*

Bagger Vance: *That ain't it. Because if you'd seen the __ wouldn't be hacking at that ball like you were chopping __ from under your front porch.*

What's the field? Fix your eyes on Bobby Jones. He's a piece of work here right now. Look at his practice run—almost like he's searching for something. Then he finds it. Watch how he settles himself right into the middle of it. Feel that focus. He's got a lot of shots he can choose from. Duffs and tops and skulls. But there's only one shot that's in perfect harmony with the field. One shot that's his. Authentic shot. And that shot is going to choose him.

There's a perfect shot out there trying to find each and every one of us. All we got to do is get ourselves out of its way. Let it choose us.

Look at him. He's in the field. You can't see that flag as some dragon you got to slay. You have to look with soft eyes. See the place where the tides and the seasons and the turning of the Earth all come together.

Where everything that is becomes one. You got to seek that place with your soul, Juna. Seek it with your hands. Don't think about it. Feel it. Your hands are wiser than your head ever going to be. I can't take you there, Juna. Just hope I can help you find a way.

It's just you, that ball, that flag, and all you are. Seek it with your hands. Don't think about it. You looking at it, Juna? Feel it.

There's only one shot that's in perfect harmony with the field.

It's the home of your authentic swing, that flag, and all that you are.

Now, here's the thing. When they made *Bagger Vance*, they made it after they read the *Bhagavad Gita*, which has this sense in the lineage of this Field, it has this sense of Unique Self—but they made it without any awareness of the meta-crisis.

They made it without any awareness of what we talked about in chapter one, when we went through the 2020s, the 2030s, the 2040s, and the 2050s and we actually saw and experienced the systems collapse—when you get to a point where you can't get a loan because the fires are raging, and no one's going to insure the shops anymore, and so there are no lines of credit, and the businesses collapse, and the financial system collapses.

As we saw, that's going to happen either in the next 30 to 40 years, or another 30 to 40 years later. David Attenborough—a pretty serious figure from United Kingdom who is completely mainstream—his prediction is that it starts in about 60 years. As we discussed before, other predictions say it starts in the early 2030s. It doesn't matter which timeline.

It's precisely accurate—I promise you that.

It's a time between worlds.

It's a time between stories.

If a new Story of Value is told, which actually inhibits rivalrous conflict, we can literally change the entire vector.

Let's remember it once again. The birds are flying in murmuration by three simple principles:

1. Fly close together with your neighbor.

2. Don't fly too close.
3. Fly towards the center.

But the *simple first principles* that are currently running the world are:

1. Rivalrous conflict governed by win-lose metrics.
2. You have no intrinsic value by yourself.
3. Your desire is somehow degraded and corrupt.

So, what are the *new* simple first principles?

1. You're irreducibly valuable and unique.
2. Your unique gift is needed by All-That-Is.

And here's the last piece. In the founding documents of the Western world, there's this notion of **life, liberty, and the pursuit of happiness.** You've all heard the phrase.

Life has great value.

Liberty—freedom.

But *the pursuit of happiness* is bullshit. When you pursue happiness, it always runs in the other direction. That's its nature. And you think, *Oh, I'm not going to pursue happiness,* but you keep looking over your shoulder, so happiness gets confused about which way you're going.

> *The only way I get to joy is if I pursue something completely other than happiness—and as a byproduct of that pursuit, I'm filled with mad joy.*

Bagger Vance was happy in that moment in the movie clip when he took his shot, wasn't he? That was his shot.

Joy comes from taking your shot for the sake of the whole.

It doesn't even come just from taking your shot for your own circle. That's a piece of joy and it's an important piece, but it's not all. I told you, I moved to St. Johnsbury for my son. I get it.

But it's not enough. It's not where we are in the world today.

We've got to expand.

Our love lists are way too short. We won't make it through the meta-crisis this way.

But when you take your shot for the sake of the whole, the byproduct is a level of joy that's unimaginable.

- ◆ We cry out of one side of our mouth.
- ◆ We laugh out of the other side.

And together, we somehow *row the boat to the shore.*

Michael row the boat ashore, *hallelujah.*

We need to know that the old song won't take us home. We're song here. That's what we're doing. The old version won't tal was based on an old story. It doesn't hold. But they got the k right, but **we have to rewrite the story.** That's what we're he ready to rewrite the story and evolve the source code of consciousness and culture.

Find that doubting voice inside of you that says that this couldn't possibly be true. Do you hear that voice? It's still there. It says, *it couldn't actually be true.* But it is. It is actually true.

And if you can let yourself have that full audacity—to know that it's not happening in Harvard; it's not happening in Oxford; it's not happening anywhere else in the world. They're not even thinking about it. It's not happening in the inner rooms of the corporations; it's not happening in the intelligence agencies; it's not happening in the governments. **It's not happening.**

One of the people in our circle—I won't say his name—he's deeply involved in the tech plex world. In the last year he has met with 90 out of 100 heads of state. Over the past few years, we've met with chiefs of staff of all the prime ministers, presidents, and heads of intelligence agencies. But they're barely thinking about it. It's barely on the radar screen. It gets a couple of hours of attention, and then the immediate press cycle takes over, and it just disappears—because there are no voters in the future. It's unimaginably shocking.

What we are doing is exactly what happened in Florence, when the Black Death swept Europe, and a few people came together in the Renaissance to tell a new story.

So, welcome to Florence, in this time between worlds and time between stories.

At the Crossing.

Amen.

Hallelujah.

CHAPTER THIRTEEN

HOMO AMOR INJUNCTION SEVEN: TAKE YOUR UNIQUE RISK

THE DHARMA OF *HOMO AMOR*

There are three things that are very core in the *dharma* of *Homo amor*.

1. The first is: *no one's left out.*

No one's left behind. No one is outside the circle. That's a very big deal because we generally form our identity by placing someone outside the circle to give us the illusion that we're inside the circle. That's how we get inside the circle. I place someone else outside, and now I feel like I'm inside the circle. I want to be in the circle, but I don't know *how* to be in the circle, so I place someone else outside the circle, or I place some part of myself outside the circle to give myself the illusion that I'm in the circle.

So, no one's outside the circle, no one's left behind. That's huge.

No one in the whole story is left behind. The 500 million people who got left behind in Covid—as so many people went on and said, *Oh, we had a great Covid, we had an awesome Covid, it was great for us.* Except for those 500 million people whose lives got utterly destroyed—but they got left behind in our hearts, we forgot them.

So, no one gets left behind. That's one.

2. Number two is: *the dharma of aftertaste.*

Moses wants to see God and God says, *It's not going to work. When you see Me, you fucking die.* Which is pretty much a biblical quote—*Exodus* chapter 33.

And Moses says, *No, no, no, I want to see You.*

And God says, *You'll see me from behind.* And Isaac Luria reads the text "from behind" as *in the aftertaste.*

This is the *dharma* of aftertaste. Meaning, *Was it great sex or not great sex?* You can't actually tell always when you're in the middle of it. You can't really tell—*was that food I should be eating or not be eating?* You know it in the aftertaste.

The truth is in the aftertaste. So just feel the beauty of the aftertaste and let the aftertaste stay with you. Aftertaste is everything.

    3. And then the third is: take responsibility for your arousal.

When we first started Mystery School, we started something called the Chung House Party. It was this wild party, stretching the limits. The entire point of the party is: *can you be radically centered and present?*

That's where a key phrase in the *dharma* came from: **Take responsibility for your own arousal.** The entire point is that *we can have this empowered masculine and empowered feminine, where everyone takes responsibility for their arousal.*

And what everyone implicitly understands at a Chung House Party is that this is part of *Homo amor.* You can't actually have *Homo amor* without the Chung House Party. It actually doesn't work. Because then it all crashes on *sexing.* The whole thing crashes.

For example, the Trojan War. Menelaus. They were just fucking everyone. It was a reason for a war.

Or, Clinton and Monica. It's terrible. It's horrible. *Let's go to Iraq and kill seven million people.* That's what happened—literally. Al Gore won the election in the United States, but couldn't quite squeak it over the line because Clinton couldn't campaign with him. Bush got in, and the war happened. Our failure to take responsibility for our own arousal—not figuratively, but literally—killed seven million people. Directly. Not indirectly.

So we need that capacity to do a Chung House party; we need *Homo amor*.

To be *Homo amor* in our Eros, in our sensuality; we need to take responsibility for our own arousal on all sides. By being in radical arousal—I take responsibility, I'm in the field. And that literally creates a new Reality.

All of the dharma is at the Chung House Party. And the Chung House Party is all of the dharma. **And there's no split between them. They're the same.**

We're all the way inside. We're opening up the source code for everyone and everything, for all future, all present, and all past. Oh, my God.

PRAYER: I WANT TO KNOW WHAT LOVE IS

We have to feel our body moving a little bit. We're moving. We're practicing here. We're getting into our bodies. We're practicing. We're moving. *Homo amor* is being born. Yes. Let's pray:

In my life there's been heartache and pain. I don't know if I can face it again.

Can't stop now. I've traveled so far. I've traveled so far.

To change this lonely life. I want to know what love is. I want you to show me.

I want to feel what love is. I know you can show me.

Breathe it in. Breathe it in. Breathe it in.

No extra words.

Breathe it in. It might feel ecstatic, and it might fe brokenhearted. **We laugh out of one side of our mouth, and we cry out of the other.**

And all the forms of tears mix into a river, and that's *nahar yotzei mi'Eden*—that's the river that flows from Eden. Completely brokenhearted. Whether I don't want to party or I am feeling madly ecstatic, beside myself. Both, and more.

So we, so tender, so slowly, find our ground. *Sulam mutzav artza*, the arch of the ladder, rooted in the ground, so we can open the heavens.

So our list of injunctions is:

4. Let your heart be broken.
5. Cry from one side of the mouth, laugh from the other.
6. Your story matters.
7. Take care of unfinished business.
8. Take the red pill.
9. Live your story.
10. Take your unique risk.

RECAPITULATION: QUESTIONS OF HOMO AMOR: WHO AM I? WHERE AM I?

So, we've looked at the questions *Who am I?*, and *Where am I?* And now it's about *What is mine to do?*

How does *Homo amor* step into action?

How is your life going to begin to look different?

We're not going to get it by speeding it up—we're going to get it by *taking it all the way inside.*

So, I'm going to throw a hard word into the space: **obligation**. Obligation is a funny word, but we have to get this word. It's a really wildly important word.

Okay, so let's play with the word *obligation*. So obligation is like a duty, something like that.

In order to engage this notion of *Homo amor*, we've got to reweave and reclaim, at a deeper and higher and wider level of consciousness, this last piece of obligation.

Let's be super slow and remind ourselves where we are. It is so easy to lose the thread. Let's just look at the question again: *where are we?* Because that changes everything.

So first, we talked about *Where?* Where are we in the world today?

Then, we widened our *Where?* to *Where are we? What's the nature of the world we live in?* Is it a dogmatic Harari world, rebelling against the old religions—doing this huge deconstructive project, but forgetting to reconstruct anything? It just says, "*Okay, it's all made up*"?

And that position has always been around. Remember Shakespeare—*Macbeth*, Act Four: "It is a tale told by an idiot, full of sound and fury, signifying nothing." *There's no plotline. It is not going anywhere.* "Tomorrow, and tomorrow, and tomorrow, creeps in this petty pace from day to day, to the last syllable of recorded time."

Shakespeare didn't accept that position, but he knew it was there.

But in CosmoErotic Humanism, we have grounded so deeply in the interior and exterior sciences that:

> There is a plotline. There is a story.
>
> We live in an Amorous Cosmos, overflowing with value.
>
> Love is not hard to find. Love is impossible to avoid.
>
> Eros is not hard to find. Eros is impossible to avoid.
>
> Eros and value are one.
>
> We live in a Field of ErosValue.

Then, we moved to: **Who? Who are we?**

We are irreducibly unique expressions of ErosValue, of the evolutionary impulse, the evolving impulse of ErosValue—and we are uniquely the expression of more God to come. There's more Eros to come. There's more possibility. It's not just value, it's *evolving* value. I am an irreducibly unique expression of the Field of Eros and Value and as such—by clarifying and living the fullness of my deepest heart's desire and awakening as *Homo amor*—I evolve the whole thing. I act upon the whole thing.

THE THIRD QUESTION OF HOMO AMOR: WHAT OUGHT I DO?

So, the three questions are: *Who? Where? What?*

So, we're now at **what.**

And the *what* question is:

- What ought I do?
- What's mine to do?
- What's ours to do?

But here's the point—that is not *an option.* That's not like, *Hey, maybe yes, maybe no.* If that was an option, it would mean:
- It's my life.
- I die when it's over.
- I chose to live.
- I decided where to live.
- I own myself completely.

And, of course, I do own myself completely. I do have the right to place boundaries. Because separate self or psychological self is real. We honor the separate self. I have a right to place boundaries. But that's just my first self.

1. So, in order to be safe as psychological self and separate self I need to be fully present and have natural boundaries—whatever

I want them to be. That's legitimate. That's real. Psychological self, separate self—that's real.

2. But then, I become mystical self. Now, I'm in the larger field, and the field is moving through me, and I'm moving through the field.

3. And then the field awakens uniquely in me. It's my higher *individuation*, my higher uniqueness emergent from the field. And my higher uniqueness emergent from the field means: **There's something that I can do that no one else that ever was, is, or will be can do—in as gorgeous, as wondrous, as stupendous, as stunning, and as needed a way as only I can.**

So that is not an *option*. I want to be super clear about that. It's not like, *Oh, I can go do something else. No, no!*

I'm an artist. Does the true artist feel like, *Oh, I could paint or not?* Does Michelangelo say, *I could have been an accountant, I could have been an artist?* Now, of course, if you're an accountant, be an accountant. You can be just as much an artist as an accountant as you can be as Michelangelo. It's not about what specific thing you do.

It's about:

* Do I do it with mad passion and mad art?
* Do I just do it for my egocentric circle?
* Do I step in and do it for the sake of the whole?
* Do I expand my field of activity to actually feel the whole?
* Do I uniquely and gorgeously impact and transform the whole?

That's an obligation.

RECLAIMING OBLIGATION AS THE UNIQUE COURSING OF LOVE THAT MOVES THROUGH ME

The crazy thing is that *obligation* has become a horrible word. It's just a horrible word. So, we need to replace it. So, in the original Hebrew, the word for obligation is *chiba*, which means—of course—*deep, mad love.* That's actually what the word means—literally. *Chiba.*

So there is no split between obligation and love. In Hebrew there's no word that means obligation. Obligation is *chova* in Hebrew, which means *love, mad love.* So the split between love and obligation, is a very strange split. So let's throw out the old meaning of the word obligation.

My unique obligation is the unique coursing of love that moves through me, that addresses the world, and is addressed by the world.

So, my unique coursing of love means that I don't just marry anyone or everyone. You're not going to do that. That's weird, right? But *why*? Because I'm drawn to a *unique current of love*, and there's a unique way that it plays, and there's a unique way we make music together. Just like this instrument uniquely goes with that instrument, right?

So, that's what obligation is. The Hebrew word is *chava*. It's a beautiful word. *Chava.*

Chava means radical, unique love. **And radical, unique love creates obligation.**

If we forget everything we did, I want you to get one sentence:

Intimacy and obligation are intimately related.

The crash of sexuality today is that we try and split intimacy and obligation. It can't be split—neither emotional intimacy nor embodied intimacy. *Intimacy creates obligation.* Does everyone get that sentence? It's a big sentence:

Intimacy creates obligation.

WHEN I PARTICIPATE IN THE EVOLUTION OF INTIMACY, THEN MY OBLIGATION EXPANDS INHERENTLY

Now, if I'm only intimate with one person, well, then I feel like I've only got an obligation to that person.

And what does intimacy mean? Remember the interior equation intimacy formula.

> *Intimacy is shared identity in the context of relative otherness and a mutuality of recognition, feeling, value and purpose.*[37]

Intimacy means shared identity. So, if I only have shared identity with my wife and my 1.3 children, right? *Me and my 1.3 children, we're really close, we've got shared identity—we're intimate.* But then my shared identity is only in that little circle. So I'm only going to feel obligation in that circle.

But if I *participate in the evolution of love*, which is the *evolution of intimacy*, then my obligation expands inherently. Not because anybody *imposed* it upon me. There was no king, and there was no government, and there was no god in the sky chasing you into the bathroom an*d banging on the door. There's no imposition from the outside.*

There's no split, says Lao Tzu, between the outside and the inside. Outsides and insides are one. The whole split between outside and inside disappears. **For Homo amor, there is no inside and outside.** That's what Lao Tzu was talking about. That's what Chung Tzu was talking about. *It's all inside and outside.*

So there's this welling up of this expanding obligation. I'm not just obligated to make sure that my kid has enough land in 40 years or that someone

---

37 *Intimacy = Shared Identity x [Relative] Otherness x Mutuality (Recognition + Feeling + Value + Purpose)*

takes over my business. I expand. Now I feel intimate with this wider circle of my whole tribe. And now I'm intimate—literally intimate—with every human being on the planet. That doesn't mean that I have an equal or exact same structure of intimacy. It means that there is an evolution of intimacy that moves from:

- **Egocentric**: Me and my peeps.
- **Ethnocentric**: My intimacy is me and my tribe.
- **Worldcentric**: Imagine the *Live Aid* concert in 1985. "*We are the world.*" It's a gorgeous moment. *We are the world.*
- **Cosmocentric**: Maybe we shouldn't have more animals in the world in factory farms than we do in the wild. Maybe I shouldn't keep a little calf for three months, stuffed up so she can't breathe, in order to have a little piece of lamb chops— while she suffered for three months—so I can have that little moment of tasting lamb chops. Maybe I'm not loving that calf. **Let me expand beyond human beings.**

I'm not just going to be *worldcentric;* maybe I'm going to be *cosmocentric.* Maybe *Homo amor* is going to look back and say: *What the fuck did we do to animals?* once we woke up and realized the pain we were causing them.

It's an evolution of intimacy from egocentric to ethnocentric to worldcentric to cosmocentric.

My love *expands.*

So now, let's move from *obligation* to *responsibility*.

My capacity to respond.

I am responsive to my partner.

I'm *responsive.* I have *responsibility.*

In cosmocentric intimacy I am responsive to the whole world.

THE PRE-TRAGIC, TRAGIC AND POST-TRAGIC MODEL OF OBLIGATION

To understand *obligation*, it's useful to use the pre-tragic, tragic, post-tragic model.

There is a pre-tragic sense of *duty, obligation,* where for hundreds of years—especially within the organized religions—you were just told what you ought to do, and it was imposed on you. For hundreds of years, that's what people's lives were like; they knew what they were meant to do.

It was an obligation imposed from outside—that's pre-tragic. But because everybody believed the source of that obligation—the Church, the Bible—there was this authority that everybody followed. That's what I *ought* to do and it brought a certain *clarity.*

But then, of course, with the Renaissance and the rise of modernity, all of that was challenged. *Yeah, but how do you have the right to impose a duty on people like that?* And out of that came the whole movement of individual rights, human rights, and autonomy—the idea that the individual really matters, that they're not just a pawn of the Church or the establishment imposing its norms on them.

But then, a lot of people got stuck in **the tragic, where *all* duty was seen as bad.** You hear this a lot, especially in the therapeutic world—as soon as the word *ought* comes back, people say: *Oh, I ought nothing!* This kind of *defiance.*

It's actually true that *I ought* should not be imposed on me from the outside. But that doesn't mean the whole concept of duty and obligation is redundant.

Post-tragic obligation means we know the pitfalls of duty and obligation— but we also see the value of placing ourselves under an obligation.

The root of the word *ligo* (in obligation) means to bind—so you are binding yourself to a commitment.

So please don't confuse the post-tragic obligation and duty with the pre-tragic that we're all trying to get away from. They're two totally different things.

Like so often with *Homo amor*, part of it is evolving into new forms, and part of it is reclaiming the old forms, but this time from a new, post-tragic consciousness.

And obligation and duty are one of those.

So, in order to be in this post-tragic obligation, I need to realize two things. The first is **the mad joy of obligation.** Just think about it. Try to access a world in which you have no obligations at all.

No one needs you.

You have no responsibility.

No one's relying on you.

No one needs your gift.

No one needs your service.

There's no creative tension that demands your response.

You are absolutely, completely free.

But you're not. You can *just feel it.* It's just so obvious. That's *horrifying.*

YOUR NEED IS MY ALLUREMENT

Let's go to the next step of this *Homo amor* practice. Now, feel **the joy of right relationship**—and this right sense that—*Oh, my God, you need me.*

One of the principles of Homo amor is: the sexual models Eros. So, one of the things that happens in sexing is:

- ◆ Your need is my allurement.
- ◆ Your need is my delight.
- ◆ You need to be felt that way.
- ◆ You need to be opened that way.
- ◆ You need to be touched that way.

Your need is my allurement. And I want to be able to be the greatest lover in the world. I want to meet your need in a way that blows your entire world open into the highest heavens and into wide and light and bright Eros. **Your need is my allurement.** And if I can anticipate your need, *wow*!

So, imagine the joy when you expand the experience of *your need is my allurement* from the realm of sexing into every dimension of life. Not just with two people, but actually, *I want to make love to the whole world.*

"As the spring makes love to the cherry blossom," writes Neruda.

I'm making love in every moment.

Reality is an Amorous Cosmos.

Lines are entering circles.

The yin and the yang dance.

The ones and the zeros.

It's all a dance of allurement—from subatomic particles all the way up, and all the way down. **And if it's a dance of allurement, it's a dance of need.** There's fundamental need.

It gets crazy beautiful now. Truth is always just insanely beautiful.

We're in the meditation.

We're on the inside.

Imagine this...

> *You're on a desert island. You were shipwrecked. You and one other person. That other person is the most annoying person you can possibly imagine. And you are never getting off of this island. It's a bad Homo amor incarnation.*
>
> *You've got all your survival issues taken care of. You've got the water, the beach, the ocean. You're good. It's been ten years. Every time this other person opens their mouth—you're about to die. But it's just the two of you on the island. Oh, my god. Horror. I mean, they're not terrible. They're just annoying.*
>
> *And then this other person on the island goes scuba diving. You happen to have had scuba diving equipment left over from the plane wreck and it wasn't damaged. I don't know how that happened but it did. And then—they're in the coral reef and they come back one afternoon and both their hands are broken.*
>
> *You happen to be a doctor. An emergency room physician, of course. And you know exactly how to fix their hands. They're now completely fixed.*
>
> *But you don't have exactly the right equipment. So, their hands are kind of straight out in front of them—in this strange cast. Two hands straight out. So, your partner can't feed themselves.*
>
> *Huh... Isn't that interesting?*
>
> *Do I have an obligation to feed them?*
>
> *No one will ever know. What will I do? I think I'll go live on the other side of the island. I'll come back in a few weeks and see what happens?*

This is heartbreaking, what I'm about to tell you. I've asked this question at the best private schools and the best universities for 30 years around the world. And from when postmodernity set in, *the overwhelming majority* of the best and brightest students fiercely argued with me and said: "You can't say there's an obligation. It's an *option.*"

Because—literally—**their teachers told them every day that *value is a social construct.*** And ultimately, that *ought* is not backed by the Universe.

Because we were so busy rebelling against the old premodern "ought" that we threw ought out. Someone even said to me, "Let's not put *ought* on the chart. People would be afraid."

But "ought" is backed by the Universe. Of course, there's a *fucking obligation* to feed your partner! Of course, there is.

Why? And here it gets really beautiful. This is a breakthrough in moral value theory. It's simple, but it's elegant and beautiful. Why is there an obligation, a responsibility, and a joy?

1. Because there's a real need.
2. Because you recognize the need.
3. Because you have the capacity to meet the need.
4. Because you're the only one in the entire world who can meet that need.

We literally just philosophically, accurately reformulated post-tragic obligation.

Joy and obligation are the same thing. That's what it means to be a Unique Self. To be *Homo amor* is: I look at the world, I don't turn away:

1. I see that there is a real, legitimate need.
2. I recognize the need.
3. I have the capacity to meet the need.
4. I have the capacity to meet the need in a way that no one else can.

But here's the last piece of the meditation: that is *mad joy.*

Remember the sexual models Eros.

Just like I have this joy of *your need is my allurement* to my naked lover, just like I have an obligation of *your need is my allurement* in sexing, **it is an obligation of mad joy in every dimension of life.**

The evolution of love is the evolution of *your need is my allurement.*

When *your need is my allurement* means that *when you're hungry, it fucks me up*—then there are no more hungry people in the world. That changes the entire vector of history. When *your need is my allurement*, there are no more hungry people in the world.

I'm *Homo amor* is not: *I went to a Live Aid concert, had a great day, and I'm back at work.* That's not *your need is my allurement.*

Your need is my allurement is: *I feel your desperation. I feel your urgency.*

We evolve your need is my allurement from egocentric to ethnocentric to worldcentric to cosmocentric.

We're intimate with the whole thing. We live in the Intimate Universe, and the Intimate Universe lives in us. It's Eros all the way up and all the way down. If *your need is my allurement*, then there are no more hungry people.

LAST STEP: YOUR UNIQUE RISK

So, I'm just going to add one more crazy sentence. It deserves much more time to elaborate on, and we will get back to it. For now, we'll just drop it into space so you recognize it when you see it.

In order to be my Unique Self and give my Unique Gift, I have to be willing to take my Unique Risk.

That's a huge sentence.

168

You can't be Unique Self, I can't be Unique Self, none of us can be Unique Self, unless we are willing to take our Unique Risk. It doesn't matter whether you're a rock star, or you're an incredible rock star gardener, or you're building houses, or you're making ceramics. When you widen and become your true Unique Self, *you have to take your Unique Risk.* **And everyone has a Unique Risk.** And everyone knows what their Unique Risk is.

But you don't know it immediately. You have to actually go inside and access—*What's my Unique Risk?*

I don't want to do things that are *foolhardy.* That's not my Unique Risk. So here's the difference between a foolhardy risk and a Unique Risk:

- A foolhardy—meaning reckless—risk; you might die.
- A Unique Risk: you die if you don't take the Unique Risk.

Literally, you go dead. That's how you know. You literally go dead. If you don't take that Unique Risk, you go dead. That's Unique Risk.

I think we have enough now to fill out the *Homo amor* chart [see Appendix].

You can just pin the chart on your refrigerator and make sure you come back to it every day. This is my orientation as *Homo amor,* with my commitment to be *Homo amor* from now on.

You can share it with a friend and meet again in the future to check up on each other. You're there to hold each other to these obligations.

YOU HAVE A UNIQUE SYNERGY OF GIFTS

On the chart you will find: *What is your unique synergy of gifts?* Your unique synergy is the unique combination of your particular gifts. It's the combination, the mixture.

For example, if your answer to the question *What is your unique gift?* is *Love*—well, that's great. But of course, that's not unique.

What's unique is your combination of gifts, the key gifts that you have.

And it's very different from someone else's combination.

Because somebody might have "love" and with that, another of their qualities might be *eccentricity* or *wackiness*. So they would spread love in a very different way than someone who had a quality of *sobriety*.

This is so crazy important and so exciting, and it's such a big deal. So, I want to just get the gravitas of this.

You may never do this again.

We may never do this again in life.

It's a life-changing thing if you do it for real.

FIFTEEN STEPS TOWARDS COSMOCENTRIC INTIMACY

Let's go gently inside. It takes something to open the door and go inside.

It's gentle, tender. So we're going to go through some of the steps we have already taken so far.

Don't read it with your mind—not even with your heart—*feel* it with your Eros, your allurement.

Because it's so crazy gorgeous.

1. We live in an Intimate Universe.
2. The Intimate Universe lives in us.
3. It's ErosValue, IntimacyValue, IntimacyErosValue of Cosmos—all the way up and all the way down.
4. The great values of Cosmos are the plot lines of Cosmos. Reality is not just a fact, it's a story. It's not an ordinary story, it's a love story. It's not an ordinary love story, it's an Outrageous Love Story. And my love story is chapter and verse in the Universe: A Love Story.

5. The plot line of your love story, of my love story, is the evolution of love. It is the evolution of intimacy. That's the plot line of the story.

6. It's not "a tale told by an idiot, full of sound and fury, signifying nothing."[38] It signifies everything. Either everything is meaningful or nothing is meaningful. And we know that nothing is meaningful is not true. So, everything is meaningful.

7. The plot line of the story is the evolution of intimacy.

8. Intimacy creates obligation.

9. Intimacy means allurement. I'm allured. There's allurement all the way down and all the way up the evolutionary chain.

10. The plot line of my story is allurement and Eros and intimacy.

11. Intimacy and obligation are one.

12. Intimacy and responsibility are one. I respond when I'm intimate. Intimate responsibility. The evolution of intimacy creates the evolution of responsiveness. I respond.

13. Another way to say intimacy is *your need is my allurement*. Meaning, in intimate relations between people, your need is my allurement.

14. Allurement, intimacy, and Eros are the Fuck of Cosmos.[39]

15. The plot line of my life is that I move from egocentric intimacy—which I never leave behind—to ethnocentric intimacy (intimacy with my tribe), to worldcentric intimacy (a broader sense of responsiveness to intimacy with every human being on the face

---

38 From Shakespeare's *Macbeth*.

39 When we talk of Fuck, in all of its expressions, we seeks to articulate a dimension of lived Eros, which is both prior to and beyond all language and culture. Fuck cannot be denied. It is a demand which, on the one hand, lives in us and, on the other hand, is sourced in forces much larger than us. Its potency is precisely in its impersonal quality. It is exactly the paradox of that impersonal quality awakening personally in us that is the heart of both Fuck's peril and power. When we choose Fuck, then Fuck becomes conscious of itself in us. This is the movement from unconscious Fuck to conscious Fuck; it is in that moment that Fuck awakens as the sacred. When we deny Fuck, then Fuck demands its pound of flesh, virtually always devolving into its more pathological forms. The sexual usage of fuck is the penultimate expression of the sense of Fuck, which is about contact and connection. It is in this precise sense that the sexual models the erotic. Or said differently, the small-lettered "fuck" of the sexual models the erotic, capital-F "Fuck" of Reality.

of the planet), to cosmocentric intimacy (intimacy with the whole thing, with the Cosmos).

I am the whole thing. I am intimate with every animal, with every bird, with the biosphere itself. I'm intimate with the biosphere. I am intimate with the whole thing.

Because it's all *Fuck*, it's all Eros.

Your need is my allurement—it's the whole thing.

And then finally, **when *need* becomes *Fuck*, there are no more hungry people.** *Fuck* **means Eros**, not fuck in its degraded form. It's Eros; it's allurement—it's allurement all the way up and all the way down.

That's *Homo amor*.

To do that, to get there, to be that, first, we have to *see* it. Now it's obvious. We just charted this path.

The fifteen steps. We're rewriting the ancient texts. It's a new Story of Value.

In this time between worlds and time between stories, only a new Story of Value—a shift in the very superstructure of Reality—can take us home and respond to the meta-crisis, like it did in the Renaissance.

This is the new Renaissance.

To do that, I have to take my Unique Risk.

Because you can't bypass Unique Risk. If I bypass Unique Risk, it doesn't work.

And here's the last sentence: *don't we always risk for love?* I just want to make that deep, intimate connection that we've never made before.

So you can just feel it.

A mad lover takes unique risks.

Risk and love are intimately related.

Not reckless, but, *Oh my God, I love madly.*

And I take the exact unique risk that's mine to win my beloved, which is myself.

So *unique risks* enter the room.

UNIQUE RISK GROUP SHARING

Participant: Yesterday, my husband and I left for a day because my 11-year-old boy had an event at school. A kind of rite of passage. And one of the activities he had to go through, was writing a poem. And the way he was asked to write a poem was picking up ten words, cut out of a magazine. Then he would put them on a white paper and continue writing words to make this poem. He was the last kid to do this. And the teacher, when he was halfway, said that he's the last one doing this, and that he's the first one doing this by himself, and that I don't need to help him.

And I saw that he wasn't writing capitals. He was making one huge sentence. And I was like, "Hey, sweetie, you can write a capital and begin a new sentence." And he looks up and he says to the teacher with this big smile, "I never write capitals. And I never use punctuations." And I could feel in every cell of my body how important it was for him not to use capitals. It was as if a shift in my system happened, that maybe a capital for him means that the first one is more important than all the others. Maybe a capital means that there is a beginning and an end, and not everything is connected. I realized at that moment, like if I obligate him, what school is trying to do, to use capitals and not write in his personal way, that I might block his way of creating his life or his way of making sense of who he is, from his insides, his obligation to bring life into form. He's a kid on the autism spectrum.

I feel so clearly it's our obligation as parents to keep the space open. So when he sees a word, he sees ten possibilities. He doesn't see just a word. So I really felt like how important it was. It feels like an obligation for me as a mom and for us as a community, Homo amor, of keeping the space open for our kids to create in the way they want.

Marc: Thank you. Beautiful. I just want to open it up just one more step. Now, imagine that I have that level of love and beauty and depth and gorgeousness and commitment to someone who's not my son. I just want to feel that. What about the kid in the poor neighborhood, in an overcrowded classroom in any part of the world, who doesn't even have a teacher who can even pay attention, who doesn't have anyone to actually stand for their ability to say "I don't use capitals." Because *every* kid needs that. And until we get to a place where every kid in the world has a parent, whether or not I'm the biological parent, we won't get home.

We can't shut off those kids anymore. We can't dissociate it from them. We can't medicalize them. We all have to be parents to all the kids. And that model of parenting, that's *Homo amor*. And *Homo amor* then breaks that model *beyond* my own son, who I am madly in love with, all the way up and all the way down.

Rob: It got to me the last half hour before we started writing, and for me it was really clear. I got something that is worldcentric, and some cosmic centric. And my unique risk is to appear as real Rob Azriel. And to not pretend, that's my unique risk. What do you pretend to be? What do you get into your head? Who do you think you are? That's quite ruthless to myself, and I feel so great, and so huge, and so cosmic. Yeah, and that's who I'm truly. Isn't that great? That is great.

Marc: I'm going to ask you not to answer this, just to take this question in. Rob and I know each other for a long time, and he's awesome, as you can see. Just think about *how does that greatness affect your decision when you're invited to step into something that builds something larger than yourself that doesn't fit into the development of Rob-ness as you see it?* That's where it gets interesting. What is this going to move you to do? How are you going to expand? And how is that wild gift of Rob going to now play in the world in this deeper, wider circle? *Hallelujah.* Amen.

Participant: My unique risk is to say no to people and to disappoint people in order to make time and space for myself and for the things I feel I truly need to do in the world. My unique risk is to stand fully in my own spirituality and not downplay it or change it to fit in.

Marc: That is huge. Everyone just find that in yourself. She just did the whole *dharma*, right? I've got to say so many "no's" and disappoint people in my circle who expect me to be a certain way in order to say my big *yes*. If I'm not willing to disappoint some people, I won't be able to show up in the world the way that I need to. It's so huge. I'm not going to hide my spirituality. I'm not going to hide, I'm going to live it large and wide. Deepest bow. Amen.

Participant: I've been born with an enormous love for life, for people, for plants, for animals. And I've been bullied for a very long time because I came too close to people. And my survival strategy became I will only show my love, my empathy, my sympathy for people if I'm invited, if I know that they like me too or they want me to hug them or go to them. And this year, I was part of the ambassadors of The Crossing, so I felt I had the invitation already to show my warmth and my sympathy and to make sure that no one's left behind. And it was so wonderful. And my unique risk is that I want to keep doing this outside of this community.

And for example, I had a talk with Wim. We met each other a few years ago, and I was always feeling a little distant because I thought he didn't want to know me. But he says, *I'm always the one who waits*. And this was so wonderful. And then Eric came to me and I said, *You have such a beautiful heart. Thank you for your warmth.*

I think that's what I was holding back. And I'm happy that I took the risk this week. And I'm really committed to be the first and not always the one who waits for the invitation. I'm going to create invitations. And not take it personally if people say, *no, thank you*, then I know it's not about me.

Marc: Just get that last sentence. I'm reflecting one sentence back just so we get it: **I'm committed to be the first and not to wait.**

Participant: I was raised in a small village with very good old-fashioned Catholic values. So my unique risk is to learn to know myself, who I really am, what are my values, and to also show it. I think that's my risk. To show who I am, my authentic self, so other people can do the same. So for me, it was really necessary to show it this moment.

Marc: If I can just give you a little tender challenge, which is: *what does it mean to show your values, how does that show up?* Just bring us in more and more. *How is that going to play in the world? How's that unique gift going to get into the world?* So we get to bask in your radiance. *Is there a way in which you're going to say hello to every cab driver?* Let us taste it. Let us see you in the world and see the world getting illuminated through you. I just want to feel it a little more. Just so we can feel it. *Homo amor*, you're gifting.

Participant: For me, it's important that all people can be themselves.

Marc: So by you being yourself, you're going to provoke everyone being able to be themselves. Amen.

Participant: I tremble and I dance. This morning, we had to be in quiet, but my beloved asked me...because when I was young, my heart was withdrawn, and he asked me, *what was the first crack in your life?* And I said, when I was, I don't know, about nine years old, and I was on vacation, and we went back from vacation from Spain or France. And we were nearly at home, and suddenly I was in a shock, because I remembered that I forgot my teddy bear. And I suddenly was in a shock, and my father said, *I will drive back.* And my mother said, *oh no, no, no...* But my father said, *I will drive back.* So my unique risk is that *if I feel that something is right, everybody can say no, but I will do it. I will drive back.*

Marc: I will drive back.

Evie: So, my name is Evie. This is emotional. I'm an emotional human being. And crying is, sometimes words that come out in a fluid way. Sometimes I can't say what it is, but it comes out in a liquid version. So, you get both now—liquid and verbal.

I work for television in Belgium, for a radio station. I have my own podcast. And my entire life up to now, I have tried to fit in into this shape that is commonly accepted. And I have never been that shape. And I have felt so lonely in my life. And I have chronic migraines and I think it is related to that. I just decided, in every cell in my body—and I'm a lot of cells, you told me—every cell wants to be me, finally. Can I be me? I grew up in a little village in Belgium with perfect parents, but I never felt that they understood me. They love me. But, and I feel guilty even pronouncing this, they are not my sounding board.

And I see that through my little daughter of seven. She's just like me. She's a sensitive, beautiful being. And my son has severe ADHD. He's just a different kind of normal. And so is she, and so am I. I am not the normative normal, but fuck the norm.

And you know, for the first time, I am doing something with the stage that I have built throughout the 20, 25 years that I'm in this media circus— because it's a circus and it's hard and it's tough being sensitive.

But now I want to use it to build something that has impact as I think it was my Homo amor. I didn't call it that way, but it's my Homo amor.

And I was so touched by someone who took the time to listen to me. Because I had a severe migraine last night, so I didn't join the party. I had my own pathetic party in my bed. I had so much pain. And he listened to me. He used his ears for me. So thank you for listening to me here.

Marc: Thank you. Amen, thank you. You begin to feel unique risk.

WE ACCESS UNIQUE GIFT WHEN WE'RE ALLURED AND ATTUNED TO WHAT'S DEEP INSIDE

Let me give you another short story on unique risk before we take the next step. Unique risk is everything. If I can't take my unique risk, *I'm fucked.* So I want to just give you an example. A short personal story, but we all have a version of it.

In television, basically, we're all checking the ratings. So in the Middle East, I started in a particular country, a national television show. We had a great slot. We had a whole team. They gave me the best producers and the best directors. We did three months of shows—and I hated every day of it.

So I fired everyone. I called up five, six of my friends and they came and joined me. I made a principle in the team: *no one looks at ratings until the end of the season.* Now, if you understand how television works—we're in the major studios in the center of the country—everyone is checking ratings every day.

So we literally threw out the ratings. And we said, *we're going to just talk from our hearts.* The show went to number one in the country. We did 70 shows. We never looked at ratings. It is actually true.

The thing that's most alluring about me and you and we is that deepest thing that says *fuck the norm.*

But not recklessly. Not irresponsibly. Not without being allured and attuned. But actually, *I'm deep inside. I'm thinking. I'm feeling. There's something there…*

That's what a unique gift means.

Unique gift means that I can actually gift my uniqueness.

And that my uniqueness is not an accident. We basically think our Unique Self humor is an accident. This is why we try to fit the jigsaw piece puzzle piece by rounding it out. But if I actually get, as a realized reality in my body, that:

- Reality intended me.
- I was actually born in the right place, to the right complex family, with the right set of issues.

And then I take my unique risk. To take your unique risk, you need to do one thing. *I* need to do one thing. *We* need to do one thing. **We need to break the pattern of yesterday.** Because yesterday doesn't determine

178

today. I can break the pattern of yesterday. The greatest slave driver in the world—the greatest *Pharaoh*—is the belief that yesterday determines today. That's not true.

Because there's not just a unique self in a person. There's a unique self of time.

And that unique moment invites a unique possibility that just didn't exist before. That new moment in time is quite literally an actual possibility of possibility—structurally, ontologically, metaphysically, for real. That unique moment in time holds an actual new possibility.

And I can break the pattern. I can rebel against *Pharaoh* in all of her distressing disguises.

CHAPTER FOURTEEN

HOMO AMOR INJUNCTION EIGHT: COMMIT OUTRAGEOUS ACTS OF LOVE

THE ONLY RESPONSE IS OUTRAGEOUS LOVE

We're going to the last injunction: *Commit Outrageous Acts of Love*. We have this huge step to take—and I don't exaggerate, I'm actually understating. We have to introduce something that's been in the space. We felt it in the space, but now we need to capture it.

It has been very delightful for me to invoke beloved Sally Kempton through her meditation. A long time ago I was teaching on Zoom at Sally's house. We were running a group called the *Dharma Circle*. Sally would be kind of doing her thing, and I would teach in the *Dharma Circle*. I wanted to do this whole teaching, but I just couldn't talk. I couldn't say anything. Everything was just so unbearably painful. There was just nothing to say.

The people on the call were very generous. They assumed this must be some profound teacher's spiritual moment where he's deep in silence. But no, I just had nothing to say. It was quite simple.

So what I'm about to tell you now just emerged in those few minutes. Because suddenly, this whole new *dharma* spilled out.

She whispered it. I just said it. But She whispered it. And Sally, who always kind of did her own thing at the house, stopped, and she took notes on the whole thing. And she gave me the notes right afterwards. It was 2011.

I just want to share with you what happened that day, in those minutes, because it's exactly where we need to go now.

The first sentence I said when I could actually say something was:

"We live in a world of outrageous pain. And the only response to outrageous pain is Outrageous Love.

That is not a cute sentence. It's not a New Age sentence. No.

We live in a world of outrageous pain. We're not interested in Jewish, Buddhist, or Hindu mystical explanations about why it is that way, which rationalizes the pain. And we're not interested in hearing that it's not really painful because we're in some bliss of True Self. We're not interested in all of that.

We don't look away. It's just the way it is. We live in a world of outrageous pain. That's just true.

But two is: we live in a world of outrageous beauty. That's also true.

We live in a world of outrageous beauty. The only response to outrageous beauty is Outrageous Love.

The only response to outrageous beauty is Outrageous Love. Outrageous love is not ordinary love. Ordinary love is a strategy of the ego. Outrageous Love is not mere human egoic strategy. **Outrageous Love is the heart of existence itself.**

Do you get that distinction? It's not a social construction. It's not mere human sentiment. Outrageous Love is the heart of existence itself. **Which is why love is not hard to find; love is impossible to avoid.**

It's actually about—*what is there underneath?* It's the allurement animating the whole thing.

So that means that I participate in the field of Outrageous Love. It means that Outrageous Love or Eros, or this yearning for intimacy, this erotic drive, is moving through me. That's what we mean when we always say:

♦ I don't just live in a CosmoErotic Universe. The CosmoErotic Universe lives in me.

♦ I don't just live in an Intimate Universe. The Intimate Universe lives in me.

It's what John Archibald Wheeler, the great physicist, called *the participatory universe.* I participate in the field of Outrageous Love.

So what does that mean?

Where am I? I'm in a field of Outrageous Love.

Who am I? I'm an Outrageous Lover. That's actually who I am. I am an Outrageous Lover.

Who are we? We're a band of Outrageous Lovers. We're not a self-development group. We're a band of Outrageous Lovers. We're a holy band.

That's what Tolkien was talking about in *Lord of the Rings,* what he called *the fellowship of the ring.* What is the fellowship of the ring? The fellowship of the ring means that in Middle Earth, when the eye of Sauron—the eye of intense surveillance that looks to dissect and to monetize and to commodify—dominates the land, and there's no force against it, **the only thing that can stand against it is this fellowship of the ring, this group that loves each other outrageously.** *Outrageously.* Sometimes one carries the ring, and other times one carries the other. Sam says to Frodo, *I can't carry the ring for you, but I can carry you.*

So *who* are we here? We're the fellowship of the ring. We're a band of Outrageous Lovers. That's who we are. That's what *Homo amor* is. We're a band of Outrageous Lovers. *Homo amor* is not one. *Homo amor* is one and *Homo amor* is a band of Outrageous Lovers.

We're not just Unique Self. We're Unique Self Symphony. When Jesus talks about "the two that agree" in the New Testament—and rabbis should always quote the New Testament and the Book of Matthew—if you look at the Latin for the phrase "the two who agree," the Latin is *symphonia,* symphony. So to agree does not mean *I nullify myself.* It means *we're in symphony together.* So, we're a Unique Self Symphony. We're a band of Outrageous Lovers.

So what do Outrageous Lovers do? Well, first, they keep every boundary that should be kept and they break every boundary that should be broken— and they have the wisdom to know the difference.

But what do Outrageous Lovers do? Outrageous Lovers commit Outrageous Acts of love—which is the last injunction. But they're not *ordinary* acts of love. My unique risk is not just *I have a unique risk in a personal development seminar to be more me so I'll be more fulfilled.* That's not what this conversation is about. There are lots of places to have that conversation and they should be had, but that's not this conversation. That's not going to respond to the meta-crisis. That's not where we are. That's not *Homo amor.*

184

Homo amor commits Outrageous Acts of Love. And Outrageous Acts of Love means for example *I'm willing to disappoint some people in order to say my big Yes.* And my *big Yes* is an Outrageous Act of Love. Meaning, *I'm going to stretch and do all the things I'm uncomfortable doing because I'm madly in love with the world. I'm committed to it. I'm going to go all the way.*

If you think you can commit your Outrageous Acts of Love and still be purely comfortable, it's just not true. I give up some comfort for the sake of pleasure.

The opposite of pain is not pleasure. The opposite of pain is comfort.

So, I give up being comfortably numb in order to get an unimaginable pleasure.

Comfort sexing is one of the terms in the *Phenomenology of Eros*[40] we wrote. Comfort sexing gets boring after a while. Does anyone know what I'm talking about? Don't answer. *Ah, comfort sexing, let's do that again. You do that, I do that, you do that, I do that, you fall asleep.* Just between us: it's boring. **So let's move from comfort sexing to *pleasure sexing.***

The opposite of pain is comfort. **There's unimaginable pleasure in Outrageous Acts of Love.** But it's a pleasure that comes from showing up again and again and again, and screaming the name of God.

Because, what do we scream at the moment of orgasm?

"Yes!"

The name of the other.

"Oh, God."

But screaming the name of God is uncomfortable sometimes, the new name of God, which is the Infinite Intimate.

---

40 The new *Phenomenology of Eros* (twelve-volume work forthcoming in 2025).

So which Outrageous Acts of Love do I commit? You commit the Outrageous Acts of love that are a function of your Unique Self. They're yours to commit. They're not mine.

FORGIVENESS IS THE FRAGRANCE THAT THE VIOLET SHEDS TO THE HEEL THAT CRUSHED IT

I want to share a story about an Outrageous Act of Love. I specifically didn't want to share it at first because it's so not easily applicable to so many of us. But I think it's an important story. To be clear, this is not the Outrageous Act of Love of *everyone*. But this is one person's Outrageous Act of Love in this particular time, in this particular place, and in its humanness.

So read this Outrageous Love Story:

> *I remember my stepfather would beat me. He would beat me with extension cords and hangers and pieces of wood and all kinds of stuff. After every beating he would tell me, it hurt me more than it hurt you. I only did it because I love you.*
>
> *It communicated the wrong message to me about what love was. So for many years, I thought that love was supposed to hurt. And I hurt everyone that I loved. I measured love by how much pain someone would take from me.*
>
> *It wasn't until I came to prison in an environment that is devoid of love that I began to have some sort of understanding about what it actually was and was not. I met someone. She gave me my first real insight into what love was because she saw past my condition and the fact that I was in prison with a life sentence for murder. Not only for murder but for doing the worst kind of murder that a man can do, murdering a woman and a child.*
>
> *It was Agnes, the mother and grandmother of Patricia and Chris, the woman and child that I murdered, who gave me my best lesson about love. Because by all rights, she should hate me. But she didn't.*

And over the course of time and through the journey that we took, that has been pretty amazing. She gave me love. And she taught me what it was.[41]

Just feel into it. Don't feel into whether *could I or couldn't I*, that's the wrong question. That is the reason why I have never used this example before. But I think it's right to use it now. And you understand why.

Feel into two things. First, feel the *fucking* Outrageousness of it. I mean, this is *Outrageous*.

But it's even deeper. You know, there's an Islamic saying, at the depth of the true holy Islam. I'm going to translate it. It appears all over literature—

Forgiveness is the fragrance that the violet sheds to the heel that crushes it.

Forgiveness is the fragrance that the violet sheds to the heel that crushes it. Now, you can't even begin to watch this or to hear this within the context of an ego self, a psychological self. A True Self just absorbs it and says *it's not there.* You can only feel this as *Homo amor*, as an Outrageous Lover.

So what Outrageous Acts of Love should I commit? Those that are a function of my Unique Self.

For Agnes, in this story, in this prison, in this place, and in this time, it was to love that beautiful man who collapsed, and to rebreathe him.

What are my Outrageous Acts of Love? My unique risk and my Outrageous Acts of Love are one. They come together. They're ultimately the same. They're inseparable.

And then, I actually re-conceive my life. Not as an ordinary story, but as a love story. Not an ordinary love story. But an Outrageous Love Story.

---

41   The quote originates from George Roemisch's poem "Forgiveness" (c. mid-20th century) and became widely known through a "Dear Abby" column. Its imagery reflects a universal theme found in many traditions.

Eight billion Outrageous Love Stories that orient not towards *whale oil,* but towards *whales*—and then the meta-crisis has disappeared.

Our crisis is a birth. Crisis is an evolutionary driver.

We're at the edge of the edge. It's not another social action program— although we need every social action program. It's not just another initiative—although we need every initiative. And you can have beautiful separate self initiatives. And you can have beautiful mystical enlightenment initiatives. But that's *not* what we're doing.

We're in the Renaissance.

We're in Florence.

It's a time between worlds and a time between stories.

We're bringing something down.

Homo amor.

It's not separate self-consciousness. It's something else. It's not my friend Marshall Rosenberg's "nonviolent communication"[42] which is beautiful— which is how separate selves get along. But that's an early reaching towards *Homo amor.*

Homo amor is a different, new consciousness.

And it lives in a *dharma*; it lives in a new Story of Value.

---

42 Marshall Rosenburg, *Nonviolent Communication: A Language of Life: Life-Changing Tools for Healthy Relationships* (2015).

APPENDIX:
HOMO AMOR WORKSHEET

HOMO AMOR PORTRAIT

	QUALITIES OF UNIQUENESS
What is your Unique Synergy of gifts?	
What are your Unique Pleasures? [Unique Aliveness]	
What are the Unique Needs of the world that can be met uniquely by you?	

What is your Unique Silliness?	
What is your Unique Fuck Up? [Pathology]	
What is your Unique Obligation? [The Four Fold Song]	
What is your Unique Risk? [Unique Transformation]	

INDEX

D

153, 154, 155, 156, 157, 158, 162,
164, 165, 166, 168, 169, 170, 172,
174, 176, 178, 183, 184, 187, 188

Homo sapiens, 8, 12, 16, 34, 44, 45,
51, 99, 107

honor, 71, 159

human, 7, 8, 9, 10, 12, 13, 19, 22,
23, 38, 42, 44, 45, 51, 52, 55, 57,
64, 76, 77, 78, 80, 81, 84, 97, 162,
163, 172, 177, 182

humanity, 11

I

identify, 59, 106, 122

identity, 11, 22, 25, 51, 83, 84, 97,
153, 161

Idra, 93

illusion, 35, 36, 71, 99, 116, 129,
135, 153

imagination, 95

imagine, 8, 15, 32, 70, 71, 82, 84,
99, 104, 105, 107, 165, 166, 174

individual, 12, 13, 17, 35, 36, 52, 55,
99, 163

individuals, 21, 55

individuation, 159

Infinite Intimate, 112, 122, 142, 185

Infinity of Intimacy, 133, 134

Inside of the Inside, 15, 40, 41, 63

integral, 28

integrating, 76, 80

integration, 1, 51

interior sciences, 15, 16, 25, 93

internet, 23, 141, 142

Internet of Things, 10

intimacy, 83, 84, 85, 89, 93, 94, 95,
134, 136, 139, 146, 161, 162, 163,
171, 172, 183

intimate, 4, 78, 83, 94, 133, 139,
161, 162, 168, 171, 172, 173

Intimate Universe, 85, 89, 93, 94,
97, 111, 142, 168, 171, 183

irreducible, 117, 124, 136, 142, 146,
149, 158

Israel, 8, 67

J

Jerusalem, 42

Jesus, 184

joy, 40, 48, 52, 150, 164, 165, 167,
168

K

Kalman, Kalonymus of Piaseczno,
40

Kashmir Shaivism, 41

Kempton, Sally, 112, 127, 128, 181

king, 120, 161

Kurzweil, Ray, 10

L

laughter, 52, 88, 130, 131, 150, 156

leaders, 3, 31

leading, 44, 60, 111

Lifton, Robert Jay, 38

line, 22, 44, 45, 65, 90, 91, 92, 124,
155, 171, 172

lineage, 40, 42, 47, 87, 93, 100, 118,
139, 148

loneliness, 115, 116, 117, 123, 155,
177

P

pandemic, 4, 16, 17, 18, 23, 25, 115

paradox, 41, 116, 130, 172

partial, 100, 143

particular, 1, 10, 11, 65, 68, 80, 81, 87, 88, 92, 116, 139, 170, 178, 185

pathological, 122, 123, 172

pathology, 120, 130

pathos, 84

pattern, 16, 32, 44, 123, 146, 179

physiosphere, 43, 44

pleasure, 21, 184, 185

plotline, 142, 157

postmodern, 67, 167

Postmodern, 10, 51, 64, 77, 109, 141, 142

post-tragic, 36, 41, 46, 49, 50, 54, 163, 164, 168

power, 50, 51, 56, 57, 66, 79, 172

prayer, 31, 32, 33, 118, 155

premodern, 51, 68, 109, 167

pre-tragic, 36, 37, 38, 45, 48, 163, 164

pride, 28, 72

process, 18, 55, 60, 83, 100

promise, 95, 140, 149

prophet, 40

proton, 43, 84

psychology, 11, 78, 98, 99, 100, 101, 105, 112, 113, 117, 120, 122, 123, 124, 133, 142, 159, 187

purpose, 10, 22, 84, 121, 146, 161

R

radical, 16, 22, 41, 82, 83, 104, 140, 142, 154, 155, 160

raison, 46

Reality, 13, 14, 28, 33, 35, 40, 42, 43, 51, 52, 55, 62, 63, 68, 69, 70, 80, 81, 82, 83, 88, 89, 90, 92, 93, 104, 106, 121, 123, 130, 137, 139, 142, 143, 145, 155, 165, 171, 172, 173, 179

realization, 12, 13, 16, 17, 25, 40, 42, 45, 51, 53, 68, 71, 77, 85, 92, 98, 99, 100, 104, 106, 109, 112, 116, 118, 123, 128, 130, 131, 134, 135, 136, 137, 139, 162, 164, 174, 179

reclaiming, 105, 164

reflect, 145, 176

relationship, 10, 11, 14, 39, 91, 94, 98, 111, 141, 165

religion, 36, 89, 90

Renaissance, 16, 64, 71, 93, 151, 163, 173, 187

resonance, 76, 94

revealed, 26

Rilke, Rainer Maria, 12

S

Sabbath, 47

sacred, 89, 92, 107, 113

sacred autobiography, 89, 92

sapiens, 9, 10, 106

second person, 109, 125

second shock of existence, 11, 13, 17

U

unconscious, 9, 172

understanding, 11, 14, 15, 19, 24, 35, 36, 37, 42, 44, 48, 52, 54, 55, 61, 62, 80, 98, 101, 103, 107, 120, 135, 141, 147, 154, 163, 177, 178, 186

unique gift, 149, 170, 176, 179

uniqueness, 92, 117, 135, 145, 159, 179

unique risk, 153, 156, 169, 173, 175, 176, 177, 178, 179, 184, 187, 190

Unique Self, 113, 123, 124, 129, 133, 134, 135, 136, 142, 144, 148, 168, 169, 179, 184, 185, 187

Unique Self Symphony, 78, 184

universal grammar of value, 88

Universe, 11, 45, 51, 64, 67, 70, 80, 88, 93, 94, 95, 122, 135, 137, 168, 183, 186

Universe Story, 51

unmanifest, 43

V

Vajrayana, 41

values, 10, 57, 59, 69, 171, 176

victimized, 23, 134

visionary, 11, 13, 35, 42, 50, 83, 97, 98

voice, 14, 23, 39, 53, 142, 151

W

wake, 18, 109

watch, 27, 187

Western, 99, 116, 149

where we are, 16, 112, 146, 150, 157, 184

Whitehead, Alfred North, 91

whole, the, 154, 162

who we are, 16, 138, 183

Wilber, Ken, 69

win/lose, 62, 65, 66, 78, 79, 117, 141, 149

world centric, 162, 168, 172

world religion, iv

World War II, 46, 76

Y

yearning, 32, 63, 183

Yeats, William Butler, 49

yoga, 78

Z

Zion, 118